CLASSICAL CIRCUS EQUITATION

Liberty, High School, Quadrilles and Vaulting

CLASSICAL CIRCUS EQUITATION

Liberty, High School, Quadrilles and Vaulting

The works of
H. J. LIJSEN

translated by Antony Hippisley Coxe
described and explained by
SYLVIA STANIER

J. A. ALLEN
London

Published in Great Britain in 1993 by
J. A. Allen & Company Limited,
1 Lower Grosvenor Place, London SW1W OEL

Printed in Great Britain

Text Designer Nancy Lawrence

British Library Cataloguing in Publication Data

Lijsen, H. J.
  Classical circus equitation.
  I. Title II. De hooge school. *English*
  798.2

  ISBN 0851315429

CONTENTS

Foreword by Mary Chipperfield   vii
Preface by Sylvia Stanier   viii

Introduction by Sylvia Stanier   I

Part One   Training horses at liberty   9

Part Two   Classic and circus High School riding   55

Part Three   Mounted quadrilles, carrousels and other
equestrian manœuvres   93

Part Four   Trick-riding and voltige   135

Glossary   163
Index   165

FOREWORD

I am delighted to have been invited to write the foreword of this new book about training horses for circus work. As far as I am aware the four small volumes by H. J. Lijsen, first published in Britain in 1956, provided the only definitive work on this specialised branch of horsemanship. The bringing together and updating of these books is long overdue. Sylvia Stanier and the publisher are to be congratulated on providing this new volume which I venture to suggest will in future come to be accepted as the circus horse trainer's bible.

Both basic training principles and advanced training methods are described logically in a most thorough, correct and easily understood manner. The wide range of photographs and descriptive drawings complement the text admirably with the stage by stage photo sequences of specific movements being particularly interesting and informative. Competitive dressage riders may be surprised to learn how little their discipline differs from circus High School riding while producers of displays at horse shows cannot fail to appreciate the detailed descriptions of quadrilles and other large arena display routines.

In common with most modern circus animal trainers, my experience has been gained mainly by assisting and watching older members of my family and other experienced circus trainers. I am sure that when I was younger reference to a book such as this would have very usefully complemented all the practical experience I was gaining. A young person embarking on a horse training career will certainly learn much from this book that can be put to good practical use in progressing the training of a horse.

I hope the reader will share my enthusiasm for this book, and for both the professional and amateur horse lover it will enhance the enjoyment of classical circus performances with my favourite animal — the horse.

Mary Chipperfield

(opposite) Mary Chipperfield and Star in performance. (David Jamieson)

PREFACE

There are many books written about training horses within the confines of modern-day competitions, the techniques and finesses of whose participants are phenomenal. However, there are few books on how to achieve results outside these spheres.

In putting together these four books of Lijsen's into one reference I am seeking to cover this much neglected area. I am not trying to compare circus with competition. They are different, yet the classical principles laid down by the old masters are the basics for all concerned. Without true basic training I believe one cannot achieve true success in any sphere of equitation.

If there is a difference of emphasis in Lijsen's writings it is the emphasis on psychology and also on extreme patience. The circus trainer has to produce horses to please the audience, who are the judge and jury combined. The detail and importance of where, for instance, a horse may or may not place his head or his foot whilst performing a particular movement belongs to the routine of compulsory tests, whereas the circus exhibition is more in line with the free style of the skater's world.

So-called 'tricks' (I prefer to call them special movements) may be, and in fact usually are, included in circus routines. BUT — and this is a big but — they should only be introduced after the horse has truly learned his basic lessons in whichever discipline of circus work he is to specialise in. I have endeavoured to describe the different disciplines belonging to each section and there is a glossary describing movements and circus terms.

Lijsen goes through all the basics thoroughly and in great detail, as well as giving instructions for many of the more difficult and spectacular achievements of the classical circus. So if one follows his instructions properly one should be able to achieve the 'trick' one is looking for.

Speaking personally, after many years in the orthodox world of equitation I find the fascination of the sky being the limit quite enthralling. However, I would suggest that one should have sound prior knowledge of handling horses before attempting difficult movements.

These books have been reprinted here from the original translation, with only minor changes to style. The illustrations with numbered captions are also reproduced from the original book; some are not of the best quality, and a small number could not be reprinted as a result. The marginal notes are mine.

I hope all who read this book will enjoy it and those who follow the instructions diligently will succeed.

Sylvia Stanier

Astley's Amphitheatre in London,
circa 1768, from the outside
(top) and the circus area.
(Courtesy of David Jamieson)

INTRODUCTION

When dealing with any subject it is always interesting to know some of its history. In the case of circus, one could go back to Roman times, when entertainment often took place in an amphitheatre or circular arena, which is where the word 'circus' is derived from. Or one could look at the travelling minstrels and court jesters of medieval times. The monarchs paid for private entertainers in the form of jesters, while the country people relied on the travelling acrobats and jugglers for their amusement. Very many circus artistes of today all over the world are in the tradition of these ancient entertainers.

The great Court carrousels, however, were largely the work of Louis XIV of France, the famous 'Sun King', who frequently held spectacular equestrian entertainments in his riding school at Versailles. In similar vein Emperor Charles VI of Austria founded the Spanish Riding School in Vienna and the Lipizzaner breed of horse. It was the age of the Renaissance, when culture was fashionable — and fashion has played an enormous part in all equestrian sports over the years, just as it has in other spheres.

In eighteenth-century England the travelling showmen and fairs were going into decline. In 1768 Philip Astley found that he could control and show off his horses for entertainment in a small area or ring. So was born the now traditional circus ring. Astley lived and worked in London, where his amphitheatre became the home of circus and equestrian drama for over 100 years.

In early-nineteenth-century France, a classical form of equestrian circus developed. François Baucher was able to show off his skills in High School riding via the circus ring. In the latter part of the century the elite L'Etrier Club of Paris was formed, where it was a privilege to be a member, and it held what might be described as mini-carrousels.

James Fillis, a British-born nineteenth-century horsemaster who used the circus ring, was so successful while working in France

1

Late-nineteenth-century depiction of the circus by the French painter Toulouse-Lautrec. Colour crayon, 1899. (Musée d'Albi)

that the Czar of Russia invited him to St Petersburg to train horses. He stayed there for over twenty years. It is for this reason that today Russian competition riders and circus riders alike still use many of Fillis's methods.

The fashion of the nineteenth-century circus is vividly portrayed by Toulouse-Lautrec in France; that of the twentieth century lovingly recorded by Dame Laura Knight in Britain.

Fashion changed in 1894 with Baron de Coubertin's idea of starting up the modern Olympic games, heralding the arrival of competition. This meant that equitation took another turn, away from entertainment as it was then known and towards entertainment with a keen competitive edge, as we know it today.

But the circus continues. One man in particular, Bertram Mills, an entrepreneur between the two world wars, brought together many famous artistes for his annual Christmas circus held in London for many years until 1967. Circuses are still highly regarded throughout Europe and the USSR, and are thriving in the USA and the Far East. So although times have changed, traditions have not.

MODERN CIRCUS

The circus is an international affair which certainly cannot be tied to any one country. Certain names are associated with certain countries, and there are families of different nationalities who specialize in particular arts.

For instance, the Chinese probably produce the world's most spectacular acrobats. If you visit Morocco, you will find 'tumblers', the people who perform multiple somersaults. The Russian State Circus covers every aspect of the circus world — horses, bears, dogs, clowns and much more.

Fredy Knie Jr of the Swiss National Circus Knie in a training session. (David Jamieson)

Stephane Gruss of Circus Gruss, France.
(David Jamieson)

With regard to horses in the circus, I think most people would say that the Swiss National Circus run by the family Knie would rank number one today. They usually only perform within the Swiss borders. The whole family (several generations) partakes in all the usual circus routines, but horses are their speciality. They use the expertise of the trainers at the Spanish Riding School of Vienna for their schooling methods. Visitors are allowed to come and watch the morning training sessions on certain days.

Circus Gruss (France) have many Liberty horses and voltige is a speciality. The German Circus Krone still use the original purpose-built circus building in Munich and have many horse acts. Mention must also be made of the Schumann family who for many years ran their world-famous circus in Denmark (now sadly folded). Individuals from the family still perform in Europe and the USA. The Monaco Circus Festival takes place each winter; started by Prince Rainier, this event still continues under his auspices, and invitations to perform there are much sought after.

Unfortunately in Britain the circus is in decline due to various

outside pressures. Blackpool Tower, home of entertainment for so many years, ceased to host circuses after 1990. Roberts Bros, the well-known English circus company, performed there in the final season. But the original brick–built circus building in Great Yarmouth is still in use.

Katja Schumann of the famous Danish circus family, at the Circus World Championships in London. (David Jamieson)

The Chipperfield family continue to perform, with horses a speciality, as do the Gandeys and the Smarts (long associated with Windsor Safari Park and currently based in Belgium). The Chipperfields run the Lions of Longleat Safari Park and Woburn Park, as well as other parks abroad. Thus although the circus artistes are traditionally travelling entertainers, they have managed in many instances to adjust to the present day and are often to be seen on television with their animals advertising products. They also work in films requiring animal acts. Mary Chipperfield's Andalusian horse, Pedro, carried the magician Paul Daniels to win the Golden Rose of Montreux television award.

Spain and Portugal have a very large number of touring circuses. The Far Eastern countries are involved in circus in a big way — Indonesia, Hong Kong and Bangkok are just a few places where

Yasmine Smart and her husband Dany César. (David Jamieson)

Geraldine-Katharina Knie, aged 11 years, riding Mary Chipperfield's Pedro side-saddle, Circus Knie 1984. (David Jamieson)

circuses are to be found. A few years ago Chipperfield's Circus took horses, tigers and some exotic animals all the way to Tokyo for a winter season there. The Sultan of Oman recently bought a whole troupe of Liberty horses, yet another indication of the very international involvement of circus.

TERMINOLOGY AND EQUIPMENT

It is often assumed that circus work means tricks, such as the horse kneeling down or standing on a pedestal on command. This is not entirely true, because in each of the circus's equestrian disciplines there is a basic routine of schooling and training. Lijsen (like many circus people) tends to use the word 'trick' where others would use such words as 'movement' or 'gait'. For instance, a small circle is a 'trick' in circus language, whereas in dressage language it would be called a 'volte' — a 6—8 m circle; in dressage competition work the word 'circle' indicates 10 m and above.

Thus in reading the text it is very important to understand that a dressage movement — such as a 'volte' or a larger circle, or a rein-back — may in this book be referred to as a 'trick'. How you perform the movement or trick is vital; in both circus and dressage the movement or trick should be correct according to, for instance, FEI rules or the standards laid down by the Spanish Riding School of Vienna.

Because a circus artiste is there to entertain, certain spectacular tricks are taught so as to please the audience, but only after intensive basic work is completed. In all the work described here, Lijsen assumes that the horse has undergone a thorough basic training. The top circus trainer is indeed an expert as well as an artiste, with immense knowledge and razor-sharp reflexes.

There are several specialist or technical words or phrases used in the text. For example, 'guider' is used to describe the smaller of the two whips traditionally carried by a trainer working his horse in hand or at liberty. 'Side reins' are sometimes referred to as 'bearing reins' in Lijsen's text; whether this is an error in translation or a genuine mistake I do not know. It occurs in the section referring to Liberty work, yet in the section on High School there is a very detailed description of the use of 'side reins', about which Lijsen has some reservations and some objections. However, he does explain how and when he would use them to obtain a result.

I have sometimes heard trainers — not only in the circus — use the words 'traversal' or 'passage' to describe a horse moving sideways, whether in 'half-pass', 'shoulder-in', 'leg-yielding' or 'full pass'. 'Passage' is the usual term in dressage competitions for a slow, elevated trot, so there can be some confusion if the terms are not fully understood.

With regard to equipment, such as rollers, ropes and hobbles, Lijsen discusses these very thoroughly, and the reader will notice times when all of these 'helps' are used and may wonder why. They can be very useful in the hands of an expert to teach and consolidate such things as kneeling or walking on the hind legs. Obviously once the horse knows his 'trick' then the ropes and so on are dispensed with. If a light touch of the stick is enough to teach the trick, however, the clever and thoughtful trainer will opt for that method, and rightly so. You do not have to go out armed with ropes and hobbles, but you do have to know your job.

To get results, you must have a firm conviction of what you want, but be careful to assess what your horse may be capable of achieving. If you achieve a little — or perhaps all — of what you want, then that is a good result; equally (but it is hoped that this is not the case), if the horse refuses to do what you want, then it is a poor result. You must go back and look to see where things went wrong and then try again, asking for a little less or perhaps asking in a slightly different way.

Part One

TRAINING HORSES AT LIBERTY

INTRODUCTION
SYLVIA STANIER

Over the ages, working a horse without a rider has been one of the arts of equitation, especially in the circus. Everyone has seen gaily caparisoned horses wheeling and turning without any apparent signals from an equally dazzling personality in the centre of the ring. It all looks so easy, and is meant to please the audience. How is this apparently effortless effect achieved? In the following chapters we shall see how it is done — bearing in mind that in whatever sphere one is working, the end result is only as good as the person who applies the method.

The reader should understand that there is a world of difference between loose schooling and Liberty work. The former requires the horse to go loose around a fairly large arena, such as an indoor riding school, with either one or possibly two people to guide the horse around. The idea is to allow the horse to relax and exercise himself without a rider on board.

Liberty work is quite different. This work is conducted in a small arena, where the horse works on the lunge line and is taught to stop, go forward, go backwards, turn and so on at the command of the trainer. Eventually the horse learns to go so obediently that the lunge lines are dispensed with and the horse goes on its own, or 'at liberty'. In some respects this is a misnomer for although the horse is loose it is under complete control and answers the trainer's commands.

Bearing this in mind, let us now examine the horse and what can be achieved from simple Liberty work.

THE HORSE

The horse is a large animal with a very small brain, but an immensely long memory. He has extremely acute hearing, eyesight and sense of smell. He responds to fear and danger by running away, but he responds very well to reward. The reward may be of several sorts: some trainers, for example, will not give their horses titbits but will pat and caress them instead. Others do give a titbit (a horse nut, carrot or sugar lump), but only when the horse has responded as required. The skill is in knowing when the horse has really tried to please — sometimes he should be rewarded for something that seems very little, but because of his small brain and willingness to please, he *must* be rewarded, rather than punished for not doing enough. His memory of punishment cannot be erased, so he will not comply any better the next time but will in fact probably do worse.

To me the most important gain from Liberty work is the absolute rapport which is achieved between horse and handler. Each horse is different and has a different reflex time. Some horses only need to see your hand move in a certain direction, while others actually need to feel the touch of the whip. The tone of your voice, the sight of the whip (or guider) and your position in the ring are all of significance to the horse. These are the aids he relies on.

The type of horse being used is relevant, as is his feeding and general care, his age and the sort of work he has done before. Excellent results can be obtained with older horses, but it is really the young horse which benefits most, because if he is, say, two or three years old he is ready and willing to learn. Horses as well as people emit body signals: just as some people are tense or

Liberty work with a Shetland pony. Mary Chipperfield and Dimple. (David Jamieson)

*Liberty work with six Lipizzaners –
Mary Chipperfield. (David Jamieson)*

*Mary Chipperfield's Friesian Liberty
horses. (Richard Tilbrook)*

excitable, so are some horses. The Thoroughbred is the most sensitive, although in the end often the most rewarding. Arabs are quick and spectacular. Spanish horses are similar, but also quiet and responsive one minute and full of energy the next. Friesians are popular in the circus world because they are very even tempered and do not get flustered easily, although they are sometimes rather slow to learn. Shetland ponies are particularly good at Liberty work (perhaps because they are too small for the average person to ride). So it goes on.

PROGRAMMES

When training any horse it is essential to have a programme of work, daily as well as weekly. It does not matter whether it is for Liberty work, ridden work or racing, although racing probably illustrates the matter most vividly. Here there is a routine of basic daily work, while the trainer's expertise is needed to assess the horse and carry out the gallops necessary to produce a winner.

What is the basic routine for a Liberty horse? I suggest that to begin with you do not let your horse loose, but keep him on a lunge line, so that he never, ever, thinks he can run away. I often use a special leather attachment linked to each bit ring under the horse's chin, so that the horse can turn without hindrance.

The standard circus ring is 42 ft 6 in. (13 m) in diameter. The smallest is 30 ft (9 m), usually used for working ponies and dogs. Placing poles on the ground to make a circle of some 13 m will help to guide the horse around. Later on, jump stands with ropes at about 3 ft 3 in. (1 m) high will make a better ring. Straw bales are also a help in making a surrounding fence. You can of course make your ring any size you wish — bigger if you have a very large horse — but remember that the standard size gives maximum control. However, you should not make any horse go too fast on a small circle, because he may fall over or injure himself by straining muscles and joints.

The first thing you do with the horse is the same as with any young horse: attach your cavesson headcollar and lunge line, and teach him to walk around you in a circle (usually commencing on the left rein). Walk up to him and halt him, reward him, and start the walking round again by stepping backwards yourself and releasing the lunge line little by little, keeping your eye on the horse's inside leg and quarters. Once the horse will walk round quietly, introduce him to the whip or stick, using it as an aid to stop and start him. Find out how near you need to be for the horse to accept the whip as a guide. Do not use the whip — or any aid for that matter — roughly or too quickly; in fact, never surprise the horse as it will only confuse him. Be clear and definite, never rough or harsh.

These first lessons should be carried out daily for between ten and twenty minutes according to results, and, to begin with, in the same order and in the same place. The association of ideas is of extreme importance.

THE LANGUAGE

I am often asked how the aids are given when training horses from the ground: what are the aids and how do they work? Lijsen goes very thoroughly into how the aids work, and he also describes in detail the correct uses of the whip as an aid or guide. The handler's position on the ground in relation to the horse is also given, and the voice aids for each particular exercise are explained.

There is no standard work on language in this sense. Although the FEI has an excellent glossary of the principal terms used in dressage, since the rider is not allowed to use the voice in a dressage test, their glossary only deals with terms used to describe movements. *The International Horseman's Dictionary* also covers, for example, parts of the horse, saddlery and different types of fences. Neither of these lists the words actually used by a trainer to influence his horse.

French is the traditional international language of horsemen, even though in this day and age German and English may be used more often. So most voice aids come from French; for example, '*Allez!*', to move forwards. You may hear a trainer say '*Allez* — walk!', meaning move forwards at the walk, or '*Allez* — trot!', meaning move on at the trot. '*Changez!*' means 'turn', '*En arrier!*' means to move backwards. '*Kom!*' or 'come', meaning to come in directly to the trainer, has a German origin.

The voice aid is very important because every circus horse must know his own name. Hence the names given are short and easy to say. For instance, at the moment I have two horses who are trained to know their names: one is 'Nero', the other 'Hussein'. The cues are 'Hoosane — come!' or 'Nero — come!' The horses know the cue and listen for their own name, so only Hussein will come to his command and Nero to his. When training several horses at once this becomes very important, because a correction should only be given to the horse concerned, not to the whole group. This is not an easy task, but a fascinating one.

In the ring in front of an audience, the voice aid should only be used as an extra aid, because the whip (or guider) and the trainer's position, plus the routine, are so well known to the horses concerned. In training, however, the voice is extremely important in producing the harmony of the whip and body position, aids or cues. The tone of the voice is also important; if a horse has tried to disobey when it is clear that he *does* understand what is expected of him, he must be scolded by a sharp calling of his name plus 'No!', that is 'Nero — no!' (or whichever is the culprit). If the horse has done well, 'Good!', or 'Brav!' in a soothing manner should be used. Each trainer will develop his own special vocabulary.

Although horses respond to certain words (and actions), it is more often the tone and the accenting of certain parts of a word which have the effect. Most international trainers know this and use their knowledge to help their horses and themselves.

THE EXERCISES

Where do I start? What can I teach my horse? I would like to teach my horse to lie down, or something spectacular like that — how do I do it? These are questions that are often asked.

The answer is first to make your horse completely familiar with the stopping and starting routine. Whatever exercise or 'trick' you may wish to teach your horse, the more he knows about the basic routine which instils confidence and trust into him, the more easily he will accept the more difficult work.

I find that there are two very easy movements to try after stopping and starting has been established. The first is a few steps of rein-back. I say a few steps because backing around the whole arena, which one hopes to achieve later, needs a supple and well-balanced horse. The second is the demi-pirouette — the horse turning to the left or to the right just as he would in a dressage test. Once the horse has learned the demi-pirouette, he should be familiar with the whip and guider aids so that he can proceed to movements like the full pirouette, and standing with his forefeet on a pedestal (which must be strong enough to hold the horse's weight and very steady). Standing on a box is of course a 'trick', but why not have a bit of fun doing things like that! Kneeling

Standing on a pedestal — Sylvia Stanier's Nero. (Sylvia Stanier)

leads to lying down, and raising one foreleg at a time leads eventually to the polka and the Spanish Walk ('The March').

Some horses are better at certain movements than others, and most develop a speciality. When it comes to walking on the hind legs, for instance, you need a horse with exceptionally strong quarters and hindlegs, to say nothing of balance and temperament. Remember, however, that you should not teach your horse to rear just for the fun of it. It is a movement which horses will use against you, especially stallions, if they feel like it.

PRESENTATION

Liberty work puts a special emphasis on the role of music and the part it should take in the proceedings. In ridden work (particularly in *Kür* competitions) the horse and rider must drill themselves to complete obedience to the beat of the music, whereas in Liberty work there may be some artistic licence. Perhaps it is best described as working *with* music as opposed to *to* music.

Lijsen quite rightly mentions music in this first part of the book only with regard to Liberty work. He stresses that a good accompanist is of paramount importance. Good tunes are important both from the point of view of rhythm and for entertainment and enjoyment. Tunes should include a good entrance fanfare. Marches and waltzes conjure up the atmosphere required, and contain good rhythms and beats. Music such as 'Lara's Song', 'Viva España', and that from 'Chariots of Fire' all help to heighten the atmosphere. (Note that there are certain restrictions of copyright with regard to using recorded music, so do check up before making your own tape.) Regarding film music, if for instance you are working with a large number of horses, then a powerful piece of music is a good idea; if the show has a Spanish theme then Andalusian music would be the order of the day. The Strauss waltzes are always popular, and the 'White Horse Inn' theme is a personal favourite of mine.

Most high-class European circuses have their own band; the tradition seems to be to have musicians from Poland. It is much easier to work with a live band than to a tape. The bandmaster's (or conductor's) job is to fit the music to the horses and their performance, beating to the time of the front feet, whereas a tape is set and there is no going back. (Metronomes are popular today as an aid to performance.) Another point to remember is that the horse himself will learn to change his movement or trick both from the 'cue' given by the handler and from hearing the music change. Most horses have extremely highly tuned senses, seeing and hearing very acutely, and they also have a memory which is phenomenal.

Presentation includes a routine or programme suitable for the horse or horses involved. Simple and correct is far better than complicated and a disaster. Leave the 'tricks' until later. It is the combination of the training, the music and the theme/dress which makes for success.

The tack used for training consists of a roller, crupper, side-reins and a simple snaffle bridle. For a smart live show the harness will be a 'number one' set which will be coloured — white, red, blue or even yellow — with diamante insets, a breast-plate and possibly coloured brushing boots. (Most Liberty horses do not wear shoes, therefore they do not need boots for the same protection as a competition horse does in lunging work.) Feathers are made into plumes which screw into the top of the bridle or into the top of the roller. This is normal in Liberty work, although you will find variations — most circus trainers are looking for something new, such as working the horse with no harness at all; but basically all the horses must be trained in a logical way such as described by Lijsen. All tack (and the horses too) must be spotlessly clean for a live performance. The horse's

Mary Chipperfield with a horse in practice harness — roller, crupper, side reins and snaffle bridle. (David Jamieson)

The same horse in show harness, complete with plumes. (David Jamieson)

colour is important in presentation: a pure white, a pure black or a golden palomino are good colours, and good red chestnuts with some white on them also enhance a show, but do not mix up the colours unless you can have an equal number of each. As well as colour, special lighting effects, such as coloured spotlights, can be very helpful.

The handler, if a gentleman, may wear a white tie and tails (no hat), or if the show follows a particular theme, such as Russian or Spanish, then he should dress appropriately. For a lady an evening gown with sequins is popular, but again the theme will probably dictate the type of clothes used.

One other point to note is that if you are lucky enough to be offered a part in a film or television commercial with your horses (or other animals, for that matter), do make sure you are covered by the Performing Animals Licensing Act of 1923 and the Cinematography Act of 1937. There is a lot of money to be made with an animal (pet or otherwise) that will do what a film or television director wants. Although this may digress from Liberty work as such, if your horse will kneel, for instance, or stand on a pedestal, or even raise his lip to 'laugh', he may be worth a small fortune.

A laughing horse with appropriate companions. Major with Linda Roberts and Jacko Fossett at Roberts Brothers' Super Circus. (David Jamieson)

TRAINING HORSES AT LIBERTY

FIRST PRINCIPLES

The trainer and his horse must be friends

There is no better way of getting to know animals than by training them. It leads to mutual understanding, a fine appreciation of animal reaction — and, you will find, it greatly improves your patience. One soon discovers that humans, too, can make mistakes.

Good, quiet training inspires confidence, for the animal learns to do what is required gradually and with ease.

Horses have a good memory for *place*, *time* and *circumstance*. These 'thought associations' play a most important part in training.

Whatever means of communication is used, you must be certain that it is meticulously comprehensible to the horse. You must be equally sure in your own mind of exactly what you want the horse to do.

Before you start the simplest training you must see that the horse is perfectly calm. No sensible person would attempt to teach a nervous, frightened child; the same principle applies to a horse.

It is advisable to run through the whole procedure and all the implications in your own mind first. Let us say that you want your horse to lie down. Think of all the things that have to be done, down to the smallest detail. Start by choosing a site, remembering that the ground should be soft and free from stones, broken glass or bits of wood. If you fail to do this the horse may associate lying down at your command with the idea of pain, thereby losing confidence; and you would have no one but yourself to blame!

Never ask more people to help than are absolutely essential, and select only those who can remain cool and calm in all circumstances. There must be no shouting, no waving of arms, no dashing about. An assistant will either help or hinder; there is no middle course. He, too, must know exactly what is required of him and the horse at all times.

Failure to make the horse lie down may be due to lack of expert help, or failing to prepare a comfortable ground site.

20

The result of good, quiet training by Mary Chipperfield. (David Jamieson)

When speaking let the *tone* of your voice express praise or disapproval. A horse cannot understand words, but he is sensitive to sound.

Think very carefully before inflicting any punishment. It is all too easy to assume that, because a horse understands what is required, no pain or difficulty will be experienced in its accomplishment.

Never debase yourself by beating your horse. Not only is it unworthy of anyone who loves animals, it is cowardly and downright stupid. No one can teach an animal which is not calm and quiet.

Always reward every effort, however small. For instance, if you want your horse to raise his leg, as in the Spanish Walk, and at first he does no more than bend his knee, be satisfied and lavish in your praise.

Introduce a new trick towards the end of a lesson, and reward the horse by leading him back to his stable. Start the next lesson with ten minutes' trotting to settle him down, then rehearse the new trick. Never allow the horse to take the initiative in heading for home: and never lead him towards the stable until he has worked to your satisfaction. If you break off a lesson while the horse is still refusing to obey, you are rewarding his obstinacy.

All measurements are given in imperial units. The size of a circus ring is approximately 13 m. The metal training rings now available are not suitable as their surrounds are too high, and an assistant cannot walk on the outside of the horse, i.e. on the actual perimeter fence. Circus rings are used by all the circus artistes, except for those working with lions and tigers who use cages. Straw bales make an acceptable ring for training, but not for public performance. Remember *not* to make a horse stand on a straw bale, as it can become entangled in it.

Fibreglass whips are acceptable, but the continental type of guiders and whips or sticks are much better and last longer.

See p. 23. A bearing rein would be used to keep the horse's head up, whereas a side rein is used to balance him with a lower head carriage. See also pp. 89–92.

Leather hobbles of a modern type.

1 The horse is made familiar with the whip. (Lijsen with Rih.)

Do not tire your horse by making him do the same trick for long periods. Regular, short exercises are the secret of successful training.

You will require:

1. A riding school or manège with a soft, springy surface. The classic circus ring has a diameter of 42 ft 6 in. It should never be less than 30 ft and must be surrounded by a low fence to prevent the animals from jumping out and running away.
2. A strong, yet soft and light, lunging rein, about 24 ft long, with a swivel at one end and a loop at the other.
3. A ring-whip with the stick 6 ft 6 in. long and a 9 ft thong.
4. A riding whip about 3 ft 6 in. long, called a 'guider'.
5. Two 6-ft lengths of $\frac{1}{2}$ in. cord, with a swivel at one end.
6. A pair of padded hobbles, $1\frac{1}{2}$ in. wide and 13 in. long, with a 2 in. ring fixed to the middle of the leather. Felt padding should cover the metal fixing on the inside.
7. A roller or padded girth with a pair of bearing reins.
8. A 6-ft length of $\frac{1}{2}$ in. cord with a 2 in. ring at one end and two others, twelve inches apart, at the centre.
9. Rewards. These are most important. Small pieces of bread, sugar or carrots (but NOT slices of carrots, cut in rounds, because they may make the horse choke).

THE WHIP

The whip fulfils exactly the same function as a conductor's baton. It is an extension of the trainer's arm which *directs* the horse, and shows him what to do. Raised in front of the animal's head, the whip means 'slow down', lowered behind the quarters it means 'faster'. So you must get your horse accustomed to the whip (Fig. 1).

It is obvious that the trainer must become proficient in using the whip. Here is the best way to learn:

Drive two nails into a wall about 3 ft from the ground and across these lay a short stick, some 10 in. long. Stand at a distance exactly equal to the length of your whip, and, *using the forearm and wrist only*, with your elbow glued to your side, try to flick the stick with the point of the thong. When you can hit the stick with ease – but not before – hang the stick on a piece of string and practise hitting a moving target. See that the point of the thong – that is the 'cracker' or short length of cord on the end — alone hits the stick (Fig. 2). You need not worry about cracking your whip, it will come naturally as a matter of course.

The riding whip, stick or guider (as circus people call it) which is used for touching various parts of the horse during training, can at a later stage be exchanged for a longer one measuring 6 ft and sometimes carrying a looped thong. This looks better during an actual performance and enables the trainer to give the horse its cues from a greater distance.

The guider is always held in the left hand and governs the forehand of the horse. The ring-whip is held in the right hand and governs the hind quarters. When moved forward towards the tail it urges the horse on: while the guider, held in front of the head, gives the horse his cue to slacken speed, to stop and to move backwards.

When not in use, the guider should be hung handle downwards from a nail in the harness room to keep it straight; it is therefore a good idea to see that it is tipped with a loop.

The lash of the ring-whip is kept greased — except for the cord cracker, which must remain dry at all times. The whip you use for an actual performance should be whitened. This is done by first sponging the thong clean (leaving the cord untouched), and while still damp applying a coat of zinc oxide mixed with a little gum arabic. It should then be hung thong down with a small weight attached to the point to keep it stretched while drying. When dry, the thong is not wound round the stock but secured by a loose knot as illustrated in Fig. 3.

2 *Whip practice.*

Today one can buy proprietary brands of cream whiteners which are easy to use.

3 *The whip. When dry, the thong is not wound around the stock, but secured by a loose knot.*

Although Lijsen has used the term 'bearing rein' throughout this section, sometimes he is referring to 'side reins'. The situation dictates the particular rein, but the idea is to help the horse to keep his balance throughout the lesson.

THE FIRST LESSON

Our horse, with legs bandaged, is ready for the first lesson. Bearing reins hold his chin in so that the line of his nose is not quite vertical, but slopes downwards and slightly out to the front. If the reins are too short they must be lengthened. The purpose of the bearing rein is not merely to make the horse look pretty. In the first place, it keeps him under control; remember that there is no one on his back. Secondly, it induces attention, for the horse cannot move his head freely and so his eyes are prevented from wandering. And thirdly, it makes him carry his head gracefully. The bearing rein is important. It should not be kept on for long periods, but you must realize that it is not used just for the sake of looks.

4 *The ring whip, held in front of the horse's eyes, gives him the order to stand. Look how attentive he is, although this is only his third lesson! (Lijsen with Rih.)*

5 *The ring whip, moving in a forward direction behind the horse, urges him on. (Lijsen with Rih.)*

6 *The horse is working his way in towards the centre. A light flick of the whip on the near shoulder sends him out to the circumference of the ring. (Lijsen with Rih.)*

A coupling can be used (see glossary and illustration), but many trainers would still normally change hands when changing direction.

To start with, we are going to teach the horse to move to the left — we call it 'on the left rein', the near shoulder on the inside of the ring. The horse, therefore, will be circling in an anti-clockwise direction. This is natural because the assistant, who leads your pupil in, will naturally turn so that he is not squeezed between the animal and the ring fence.

You, the trainer, stand in the middle of the ring, holding the lunge in your left hand. Do not wind it round your wrist, as this can be dangerous. In your right hand you hold the whip.

While the horse moves round the ring as near to the fence as possible, you will describe a small circle near the centre, holding the lunge well off the ground, keeping your position behind the horse's eye, and pointing the whip at his shoulder. If you get dizzy, you can vary your walk from time to time by following the sides of a small imaginary square.

If the horse moves too slowly, move the whip behind the horse, but do not touch him with it. The whip should never come into contact with the hind quarters because this may make a horse kick. If the whip has to be used at all the thong should be thrown so that it just reaches the near side of the body at a point a little behind the shoulder.

After the horse has made a number of circuits satisfactorily, you say 'Halt!' or 'Ho!', calmly raising your whip in front of his head and giving a series of short tugs on the lunge until he stops (Fig. 4). Directly he comes to a halt, caress him and give him a reward. He must not be allowed to move forward until the whip is lowered, and the command given to move on (Fig. 5).

In order to make our wishes perfectly clear, it is worth while employing an assistant for the first lesson, walking at the horse's head. The assistant will help to keep the animal out near the ring fence, but if at any time the horse shows a tendency to work in towards the middle, flick the near shoulder with the thong of the whip (Fig. 6).

Next repeat the lesson so that he learns to travel 'on the right rein', that is with the off side facing inwards, or moving in a clockwise direction. The lunge is still held in the left hand, the whip passing under it. You will find it a help to join the two snaffle rings under the chin with a short length of string on which a 2 in. ring has been threaded; to this is clipped the lunge. It will save you shifting the lunge from one side of the bit to the other every time you change direction.

Do not imagine that because your horse has mastered a movement on the left rein, he will automatically do it on the right rein. Every movement has to be taught on each rein.

To drop from a trot to a walk, you give the animal the same cue as that used to bring him to a halt when walking. It is a little more difficult, but your pupil will soon learn.

Always give the same orders in the same tone of voice.

THE CALL

To teach a horse to come to you when called (Fig. 7), first get him walking quietly round the ring on the left rein. (All new tricks are first introduced when the horse is working in this direction.) Then you must gradually increase your own circle, moving away from the centre towards the horse, taking up the slack in the lunge as you go, until you are walking parallel to the horse about one and a half yards away from him.

Next, incline inwards towards the horse, bring the whip over to the left, pull the lunge to the right, stop, give him his cue by quietly calling 'Come' or 'Here', and slowly walking backward towards the centre of the ring. You must see that you walk more slowly than the horse so that he comes right up to you. Then stop and caress him. After this, move backwards in various directions urging the horse to follow you closely. Every so often stop, caress him and give him a reward. In this way you can teach the horse to follow you whenever you move backwards.

When you want the horse to circle the ring-fence once more, move your whip to the right, shift your own position a little to the right so that you are by the near foreleg then point the whip at the near shoulder and urge the horse forward; while doing this, take a few steps forward and slowly turn to the left.

Repeat the exercise at *irregular* intervals; but during the first lesson give the horse his cue when he reaches the same spot. If you were to repeat the trick at *regular* intervals, the horse would soon take the initiative and come to you without being told! If the horse does come to you when you do not want him, do not reward him; but do not punish him either. Just start all over again by taking him back to the circumference of the ring.

As soon as the horse understands, you can give him his cue at a greater distance. Eventually he will come when you cue him from the centre of the ring: and then he should walk towards you

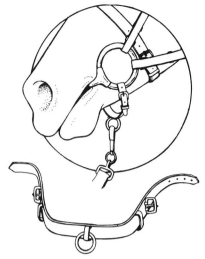

Leather coupling behind the bit.

7 My Liberty and High School horse Othello always comes when called, even when he is out at grass. (Lijsen with Othello.)

The circus horse must learn both to stand out on the track and to come in when called.

8 My horse, moving on the left rein, must now learn to change direction. The left hand brings the lunge over to the right, while the whip prevents him from coming up on my left. The horse follows his head, and turns to pass in front of me. I then take a step forward and point the whip at his off shoulder, while the lunge keeps his head up to the right. (Lijsen with Rih.)

Clarity of command is essential. Start with standing out on the track, and when that is established (some days later) ask for 'Come', and then (some days later) '*Changez*'. Thus the horse knows exactly what you mean by each command.

The aids or signals (cues) are given by voice, by body movement and by the use of the whip and guider. Each horse will vary as to how much emphasis needs to be put on any one of these aids, but they must be used in harmony.

---

when, after calling while taking a few steps backward, you then stand still.

This lesson must be given on both reins. Obviously on the right rein all side movements will be made in the opposite direction.

This is a most important exercise — and it must be thoroughly rehearsed. The horse must learn to pay great attention to the whip.

During the early stages it may again be found useful to call in an assistant who, in moving behind the horse, urges him towards you.

CHANGING DIRECTION

Your horse has now learnt to come when called. The next trick is to change direction. Suppose he is walking on the left rein and you want him to walk on the right rein. What you must make him do is:

(a) Come to the centre;
(b) Pass in front of you;
(c) Move to the right.

He has learnt to come to the centre at the command 'Come!' or 'Here!' You must now say 'Change' or '*Changez!*' and stand waiting for him in the centre of the ring. As he approaches you must quietly take one or two paces towards him, keeping slightly on his off side, moving the right hand to the left and touching him with the whip on his off shoulder; thus urging him forward and to his left, so that he passes in front of you and then away to your right (Fig. 8).

If you compare the two lessons of the Call and the Change, you will notice that not only does the spoken cue differ ('Here!' or 'Come!' in one case, 'Change' or '*Changez*' in the other) but the trainer's movements also differ. In one he remains standing still, in the other as the horse approaches the centre of the ring he must move towards him forcing him to pass and so change rein. These two fundamental tricks must be well rehearsed before passing on to others.

Never do away with the lunge until the trick is performed perfectly. Do not cue the horse either regularly or when he reaches the same spot. If you do, he will associate the place and not your voice or movement with the action he is required to do.

KNEELING ON BOTH KNEES

As you can see from Fig. 9, for this trick the horse wears padded hobbles with the fastenings on the outside and the rings at the back. The 6 ft length of cord with the three rings attached is now placed round the surcingle so that the two rings in the centre come under the belly of the horse just behind the forelegs. The plain end of the rope is then passed through the ring at the other end and secured by a loop-knot *which can easily be pulled undone* on the near side of the withers. The two short lengths of cord are clipped on to the two rings and each led down through the ring on its respective hobble from the inside outwards and back through the ring to which it is clipped.

You really need two assistants to help you with this trick, one standing on each side of the horse, level with its shoulder; here they must remain, whatever happens. The one on the near side holds the horse's rein in the left hand and the cord leading to the horse's near hobble in his right. The assistant on the off side holds the rein in his right hand and the cord leading to the off hobble in his left. The horse is so placed that he cannot move backward, and it is the assistants' job to see that he does not jump forward.

See that the ground immediately in front of the horse is really soft; cover it with straw if necessary. Kneepads can be worn as long as the joint can move freely.

You, the trainer, stand facing the horse and a little to the left. To stand directly in front is dangerous because the horse may jump forward. You gently tap the near foreleg on the front of the cannon. After a while the horse will raise his leg, then — but only then — must the assistant take advantage of this by pulling gently but firmly on the cord, thus keeping the leg bent. He should talk soothingly to the horse all the time, and hold the leg up by the cord until you tell him to let go. You next tap the off foreleg, still standing slightly to the left of the horse, and the exercise is repeated.

As soon as the horse reacts immediately by raising its leg when touched, you must quickly touch the other leg, and directly this is raised the horse naturally drops on to his knees. At this point the horse will probably try to jump up. This must be prevented by the two assistants keeping the horse's head low. The horse will very soon understand what is wanted, and remain on both knees.

9 My horse is receiving his first lesson in kneeling. He has already raised his near foreleg on being tapped, and my assistant is keeping it up by means of a hobble cord. (Lijsen with Pollux.)

It is also dangerous to stand in front of the horse as he may strike out with a foreleg.

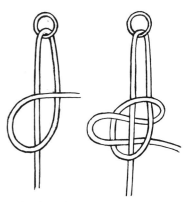

Quick release knot.

Kneeling on both knees, head and neck stretched out. Mary Chipperfield and Star. (David Jamieson)

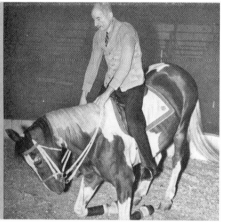

10 Here is a Liberty horse kneeling for the first time when mounted. In order to keep the horse straight the reins are held in both hands. (Lijsen with Pollux.)

When rehearsing this trick never forget to speak in a soothing voice to give him confidence. Directly he remains on his knees — even if only for a moment — give him a reward, say 'Up!' and at the same time (but not a moment before) pull the loop knot, thereby loosening both hobble cords at once. After a few lessons the assistants can loosen their individual cords at the command, 'Up!' By this time the horse should remain perfectly calm. But to start with, unless your assistants really know what they are doing, let go the encircling cord yourself — it's much safer!

Never allow the horse to get up before you give the command. Never work this trick more than once in any one lesson. Never hurry. Never let the assistants pull the leg too high, the horizontal position is quite high enough. Take your time, and your horse will soon learn, especially if he is ticklish!

Some horses, especially those who suffer from a sore back (for whom, incidentally, kneeling is an admirable exercise), find it difficult to kneel. With such animals you must be particularly

Mary Chipperfield training Spot to lie down and sit up again. (David Jamieson)

patient. Be content with the slightest effort they make, reward them, and go on practising. Success will come in the end (Fig. 10).

LYING DOWN

Good training is always logical. As a matter of fact training must always be good otherwise it is not training at all; it is cruelty. This should be constantly borne in mind.

How does a horse lie down? If you watch, you will see that first he kneels, then falls on one shoulder. Your horse has already learnt to kneel to order, but we must now see that he always falls on the same shoulder, the near one. This is most important. All horses have a favourite side on which they lie, and if this should be the off we may encounter some difficulty, but for these horses it is a particularly good exercise.

The horse is brought into the ring and harnessed as for the previous lesson, except he carries no bearing reins. We need only one assistant who stands at the near side of the horse holding both hobble cords in his right hand and the snaffle rein in his left. Since we want the horse to fall to the left the quick-release knot must be tied on the off side (Fig. 11).

First you give the order and cue to kneel, using the guider held in the left hand to tap both legs just below the knee at the same time. Next, taking up a position behind the assistant, seize the right rein and pull the horse's head downward and sideways. Don't hurry. Take your time.

When the horse falls on to its near shoulder, caress him and give him a reward at once, and after a moment or two give the order 'Up!' releasing the cord as before (Fig. 12).

11 Pollux kneels, stretching his neck over Castor's body as he lies on his near side – a position known as 'the camel'. (Lijsen with Castor and Pollux.)

12 Othello is lying down while Paul, the pony, places his forelegs on the horse's side, and waits for his reward. It is better to use some form of cushion during the initial stages of training a horse to do this trick. (Lijsen with Othello and Paul.)

Two young horses, having learnt to kneel on one knee individually, carry out their trick at the same time. Note that each horse has the opposite leg stretched. (David Jamieson)

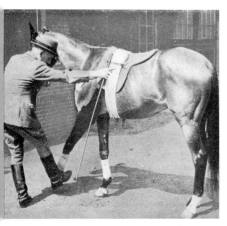

13 In getting a horse to stretch his leg I place my foot in the hollow of the heel and hold it there until he puts his weight on it again. (Lijsen with Pitschourikian.)

Horses who usually lie on their right side will protest to start with, but if you remain quiet and confident, as in the kneeling lessons, you are sure to succeed. Even if in the beginning your horse lies like a cow you must be satisfied. As you make him fall to his left touch him with your stick on the near shoulder.

Eventually you will cue the horse to lie down in two distinct movements:

(a) Touch both cannons simultaneously giving the order 'Down!'
(b) When kneeling, touch the left shoulder.

After a little practice you may find that the horse will lie down when really all you want him to do is kneel. This must be corrected. He must get no reward, and he must be made to get up at once and start all over again until he does the trick properly.

Only one lying-down exercise should be performed, and at the end of the lesson.

KNEELING ON ONE KNEE OR CURTSY

This is the trick used when horses take their bow, called on the Continent *la révérence*.

When the horse has learnt to kneel on both knees he will of course bend both legs when the order is given. You must therefore teach him to bend only that which is tapped with the stick.

Now, which knee ought to be bent? The answer is that for a school horse it should be the off knee and for Liberty horses the near knee, because in the circus the trainer usually stands on the near side of the horse he is presenting.

Your horse will be harnessed very much as before; but, on the leg which has to be stretched out in front, the hobble is attached so that, although the fastening still comes on the outside, the ring is in front. On the leg which has to bend the ring naturally remains at the rear.

You will need two assistants, one to see that the off leg is stretched to the fore and the other to see that the near leg is bent. Before you give the order and cue to kneel, see that both forelegs, while remaining close together, are stretched out as far from the hind legs as possible. Then, while the off leg is kept outstretched, the horse is made to bend the near, while you take hold of both bearing reins and urge the horse backward. At first the horse may find it difficult to get his knee on the ground, but he will succeed in time.

14 Kneeling on one knee. The reins are held in the left hand, leaving the right free to tap the front of the cannon. (Lijsen with Favori.)

You can teach him to stretch his legs out to the front, by urging him to lift a leg and at the same time pressing your foot into the hollow of the heel so that he moves it forward (Fig. 13). Do this to each hoof alternately, always giving the order, 'Stretch!'

The final accomplishment of this trick can be achieved by a different method to that first described. As soon as the horse has learnt to keep both legs stretched out in front, pass both reins between the forelegs, and, stooping down at the side of the near knee, offer the horse a reward between his forelegs from behind. Then the leg raising must be learnt, the horse being tapped on the cannon, and the reward given.

Gradually — very gradually — move the reward further back. Progress here must be made very slowly, so do not attempt to hurry. Without patience you will fail. But if you take your time and try to see things through your horse's eyes, you are sure to succeed (Fig. 14).

PIROUETTE WITH CROSSED FORELEGS

There are various ways of teaching a horse this trick (Fig. 15). Sometimes a stick is placed between the forelegs, but the simplest and easiest way is as follows.

What we have to do is to get the horse to move his quarters round the forelegs, which must remain in exactly the same position

15 Pirouette with crossed forelegs. The horse has completed one turn and is about to move in the opposite direction. (A. van Os.)

The lunge rein correctly fitted to teach the pirouette with crossed forelegs. The assistant must hold the other end.

so that they become crossed as the quarters swing round. Bearing reins are fixed in position. His two fore-hooves are close together and side by side. Now take a short lunge, fold it in two and slip it round the forelegs in a noose. During the early lessons see that this noose is not too tight (Fig. 16).

You must next persuade your horse to turn his quarters sideways, by touching him with your stick. If the forelegs remain still for no more than a few paces, be satisfied, stop and reward him. If he moves them — start all over again and talk to him in a gently reproving tone, as you should always do when he makes a mistake.

It is best to stand at the horse's head; and, if it is your intention to make the quarters travel in an anti-clockwise direction, hold the left bearing rein and the lunge which is wound round the forelegs in the left hand, and your stick or whip in the right.

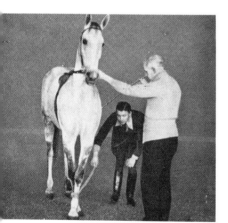

16 Pirouette with crossed forelegs. The lunge is looped round the legs in a noose, keeping them together. (Lijsen with Tancret.)

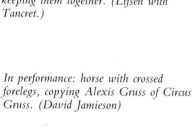

In performance: horse with crossed forelegs, copying Alexis Gruss of Circus Gruss. (David Jamieson)

Give the command 'Turn!' and touch the near hind leg with the whip. If he tries to move his forelegs stop. And if he tries to move quickly, stop till he calms down.

The number of steps which your horse takes will grow until he eventually completes the pirouette. Leave the lunge round the forelegs until you are quite sure he will keep them still.

STANDING ON THE HIND LEGS OR REARING

This is a trick which one horse will do quite naturally and another will never learn. Your horse should be bridled with bearing reins and snaffle to which a short lunge is fixed on either side held by an assistant. The trainer stands in front of the horse with his whip in his right hand and a leading rein attached to the nose-band in his left. Another assistant with a whip stands behind the horse. The horse, therefore, cannot move backward, forward or sideways.

When you give the order, 'High!' (not 'Hup!' which is too like the sound associated with rising from the kneeling position), the rear assistant urges the horse forward and you touch it under the chin with your guider. Under no circumstances must the horse be allowed to fall back (Fig. 17).

Directly he raises his forelegs off the ground — if only for a split second — he must be fondled and rewarded. This is repeated three times during each training period, but the horse must be absolutely quiet before you start. The horse will soon understand, and one day he may even start to rear before the order is given.

17 Hans Strassburger brings his troupe of Frieslands up in a rear.

In other words, he must not be allowed to step backwards.

Mary Chipperfield and two assistants teaching the horse to rear. Note that the trainer has two whips and the assistants a lunge line each. The horse is placed with its back to the ring fence. (David Jamieson)

Sometimes two assistants are enough, one to stand either side of the horse's head, with the trainer in front. The horse can be backed up to the fence so that he cannot step backwards. A third assistant can help by picking up a foreleg with a rope around the pastern, to encourage the horse to go up on command. He must *never* be allowed to rear in defiance or as a resistance.

18 One of my ponies walking on its hind legs. (Lijsen with Mikado.)

Pedestals are usually between one and two feet high and made of very solid wood.

This must be stopped immediately. *You*, the trainer, alone must give the order, and you must never allow the horse to take the initiative. So, keeping your whip pointing at the ground, you give him no reward but gently reprimand him until *you* give the order, then if he obeys he is rewarded and petted at once. If he is slow to understand the command, 'High!', an assistant should raise the foreleg, and keep it bent while you give the cue.

If he rears incorrectly, we must put matters right, *but not until he will rear to order*. Then, if he throws his head too high, use a martingale just long enough to keep his head in the correct position; if he kicks out with his forelegs, tap him on the cannons with your whip.

Again be satisfied with little, and keep the lessons short (Fig. 18).

FORELEGS ON PEDESTAL

Your horse must, of course, become perfectly familiar with the 'props' you expect him to use. Horses that shy should never be hit: after all they are not doing anything wrong. When you show your horse the pedestal for the first time, don't trundle the tub you are going to use towards him; leave it lying in the ring before you bring the horse in and lead him slowly and quietly up to it, talking soothingly all the time. Then place a piece of bread or carrot on the pedestal and let him eat it off the top. See that he gets quite used to the tub before starting to train him.

Next put the hobbles on the forelegs with the rings to the fore, and a short lunge attached to each ring. Place one leg on the pedestal and make him keep it in this position while you pet and

A pedestal with a central handhold for carrying, and how to make it so that it is sufficiently strong. The measurements are approximate.

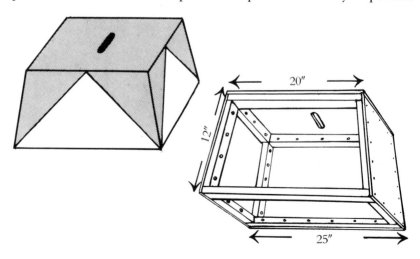

praise him. As like as not he will put the other leg up of his own accord. If he doesn't, then during the first few lessons your assistant must put it up for him.

When he is completely at ease in this position, loosen one bearing rein, move round to the other side and hold the rein which is still attached. Then make the horse move his hind quarters round in a circle away from you. His forelegs, of course, stay on the tub, shifting position for comfort. Then try the same movement in the opposite direction.

Teaching a young horse to stand on a pedestal, with a reward for performing correctly. (David Jamieson)

The horse is given the usual 'Come' instruction (see p. 25). In the beginning the trainer (or his assistant) will have to place the horse's foot on the pedestal as the command to mount is given.

A circus ring fence is approximately 18 in. high and 18 in. wide, so that a person can walk on it. It must be solid enough to take the weight of the horse's feet as well. It is made up of sections, two of which can be opened and shut to form the entrance (see illustration on p. 51).

Remember that the correct whip training should be given right from the beginning (see p. 24).

Finally, place the tub in the centre of the ring, while the horse is present. Stand on the far side and, keeping the tub between you and your horse, call the horse to mount and pirouette. You will now follow the quarters as they move round.

FORELEGS ON THE RING FENCE

Get your horse to trot anti-clockwise round the ring; give the order to halt and raise your whip so that the thong moves vertically upwards in front of him. Directly he stops, take a step forward, flick the whip behind the near foreleg, and at the same time get your assistant, who should be standing outside the ring, to take the off rein and urge him to place his forelegs on the ring fence (Fig. 19). Keep the thong of your whip moving upwards until he stands still in the required position. Then hold the whip high, as you should always do while your horse is standing still to order.

19 Six horses, six zebras and six ponies walking with their forelegs on the ring fence. The ponies are descended from the King of Hanover's stallions. (Lulumann Gautier.)

When you want the horse to drop back into the ring, take a pace back towards the horse's tail, and order him to move on while your assistant presses his head in slightly towards the centre of the ring.

If you want your horse to walk with its forelegs on the ring fence (Fig. 20), first make him stand in that position, then take a pace to the rear and urge him on, but this time you keep the guider in your left hand held fairly high; this should make him keep his forehand on the ring fence. The whip, held in the right hand, is moved from right to left and the assistant, with his hand on the rein, urges the horse forward and not inward. He must also see that the animal's hind legs remain in the ring.

Be satisfied with a few steps, then stop and repeat the movement.

20 *Four horses walking on the ring fence. This photograph is particularly interesting as it shows that in spite of the bearing reins they look ahead along the line of movement. (A. van Os.)*

You may find it best to leave the bearing rein loose for the first few lessons.

Very soon your horse will place its forelegs on the ring fence and keep moving. When you want him to drop back into the ring, however, it is best to make him stop before giving him the order to come down, until the day arrives when he combines these actions of his own accord.

When teaching two or more horses to follow this routine together, see that they remain close to each other. If one lags behind, stop the front one until the others have caught up. To try to speed up a slow horse while those ahead are still moving is bound to end in failure.

PEDESTAL MOUNTING

To get all four legs on to the pedestal, as in Fig. 21, the hobbles are fastened round the hind legs, which can then be drawn very

Make extra sure you are using a big enough and strong enough pedestal, and that the horse has no objection to it.

21 *My pony Paul stands with all four feet on a pedestal. It was not easy to teach him to do this because the tub was rather high. I therefore fixed an old motor tyre round the tub, halfway up, to help him in the first lessons. (Lijsen with Othello and Paul.)*

carefully on to the tub. When the horse has three legs on the tub the fourth tends to follow quite naturally; you must however control this movement as your horse may not lift his leg quite high enough. As soon as he is up on the pedestal you ask him to turn round (pirouette) while you walk round at his head holding the bridle in one hand. When you order your horse down, stop him as the forelegs reach the ground. You can then teach him to move round while his hind legs remain on the pedestal.

HIND LEGS ON PEDESTAL OR RING FENCE

Bring your horse into the ring, wearing the hobbles on his hind legs. Make him stop and get your assistant to place the off hind leg on the tub, using a short cord attached to the hobble. This done, let the horse rest a moment or two, caressing him the while. Your second assistant now lifts the other hind leg on the tub, so that both hind legs are on the pedestal and both forelegs are on the ground. If you have no second assistant, then your first assistant must let go of the off hind hobble, passing in front of the animal, move round to lift the near hind leg, while you press the horse's head a little to the right.

When both hind legs are on the tub caress and reward your horse, while he remains in this position for a few moments. Then the hobble cords are removed, he is walked round the ring, and the lesson is repeated at the same spot. The pedestal should not be placed in a different position until the horse understands thoroughly what is required.

You can, of course, use the ring fence in place of the pedestal.

Your aids or cues are as follows:

Hold your stick high in front of the horse's head and say 'Ho!' to make him stop.

Pull the lunge, which you should always use when you are too far away from the horse to reach his head, gently towards the centre of the ring, and at the same time move the whip from right to left, urging the horse forward. Since we have him held by the head and in a halted position, this invites him to move his hind legs out and therefore up on to the ring fence.

Once the hind legs are on the fence the stick points towards his eye, and the whip towards his tail.

When we want him to get down we drop the point of the stick.

Fig. 20, showing horses with fore and hind legs alternately on

The stick used should be the guider.

the ring fence, is particularly interesting. Note that a horse must look in the direction he is moving, owing to the strong thrust of the quarters, and note particularly that the hind legs hug the ring fence. This is important as most amateur trainers allow the hind legs to stray away from the fence. This makes it very difficult for the horse to move forward.

OBEISANCE (*Bowing with the head lowered through the forelegs*)

This is the position known as *plié* (Fig. 22). The horse with hobbles fastened round the forelegs, but no bearing rein, comes to the centre of the ring. Your assistant should hold the cord attached to the hobbles. All he has to do is to see that the horse's fore hooves remain level and sufficiently far apart for the horse to get his head between his legs.

22 *Hans Strassburger presenting a stallion in the plié position. The horse bows so low that the back of his forearms almost touch the ground. (Hans Strassburger with Boy.)*

You stand at the horse's near shoulder with a short lunge fastened to the back of the noseband and passed between the forelegs. First you must get your horse to stretch, by making him move his hind legs and body backward while his fore hooves remain in the same position. Then repeating the word 'Bow!' you offer him a titbit from the rear, your arm passing between the forelegs from behind. At the same time you pull on the lunge to make him lower his head. The slightest movement in the right direction is immediately rewarded, and at each attempt you must try to get his head a little lower and further back (Fig. 23). But do not ask too much of your horse; the trick is difficult and can even be dangerous. Horses have torn their peritoneum when the trainer has tried to make the horse go too fast or too far.

Sometimes a horse will learn this movement simply by being tempted with a carrot or other tit-bit held centrally under his stomach, without requiring hobbles or the lunge.

When the horse really understands the movement, you can fasten the bearing reins, but *don't keep them too short.*

SPANISH WALK

A horse that has been well trained is easily handled, for in learning a variety of tricks it has gained confidence. Some of the tricks, moreover, are really useful. Kneeling on both knees for instance is a splendid exercise for horses with sore or weak backs. And the Spanish Walk is the remedial movement I teach all horses that are stiff in the shoulder and whose trot and walk are therefore too short.

23 *A piece of sugar offered from behind induces this mare to lower her head between her forelegs. (Colonel Schmidt with Lady.)*

The movement can be achieved in various ways. For instance, having attached hobbles, rings to the front, on the forelegs, your

24 In teaching the Spanish Walk I first touch the foreleg as high as possible. The horse merely lifts his leg — but I am satisfied, reward him, and start afresh. (Lijsen with Pitschourikian.)

I also prefer this method when working from the ground.

In other words, the assistant should put a rope or hobble around the pastern and pull the leg as described.

assistant can pull the leg *up* and *out*. On no account should he pull *out* and *up*; this is most important.

Here are the full instructions. First, tap the leg, *as high up as possible*, until it is raised (Fig. 24). As soon as the leg has left the ground, *but not before*, the assistant pulls the leg up and then out as far forward as possible. You can then caress the horse and move on, repeating the movement. Each leg is treated in the same manner.

As soon as your horse has grasped what is required you ask it to raise his legs *in succession*. If you have a third assistant he should be stationed behind the horse to touch the back of the cannon of the hindmost leg at each step.

Remember to keep your horse moving.

Personally, I don't care for this method and so employ a rather different technique. Here it is.

I tap the foreleg, as high up as possible, until it is raised, *no matter how little*, and then caress the horse and walk on. Soon my horse paws the ground to order. At this point he is made to take a quick pace forward by touching him on the girth as soon as the leg is extended.

Some horses persist in bending one leg. It may then be advisable to use a lunge as described above. The hind leg should always move with the opposite foreleg.

Teaching the Spanish Walk, or 'March'. Note that the position of the lunge line and the whip is as in illustration 24. (David Jamieson)

Recently one or two books have been published which contain the most misleading illustrations of the Spanish Walk. In these the foreleg may be shown fully extended, but the rein is long, the nose outstretched and the hind legs are motionless! This is just about as far removed from High School as possible.

The basic principle underlying all aspects of equitation is *eagerness to move in the intended direction*; if this 'impulsion' is missing and the horse is not on the bit, the whole performance is valueless.

Although in this exercise your horse is not being ridden, he must still be on the bit in the Spanish Walk, carrying his head in the correct position. His movements must be lively, the foreleg and the opposite hind leg moving almost simultaneously. The correct carriage of the head should be the result of a lively gait.

Even in the Spanish Walk the desire to move forward comes first, and extending the leg second.

PEDESTAL TURN WITH JAMBETTE (Outstretched leg)

By now you will have taught your horse to turn with his forehand on a pedestal, and he also knows the cues for extending the forelegs, although only when walking. You are going to combine these two exercises, as in Fig. 25, and with this in view he is made to put his forelegs on the pedestal.

25 Jambette on pedestal. The near leg ought to be nearer the centre of the tub. (Colonel Schmidt with Lady.)

First he must be taught to extend his leg. For this you will need a hobble with the ring at the front and the fastening to the outside. Attached to this is a short cord held by your assistant. You must stand on the off side with your left hand on the bearing rein, and in your right you carry a stick. You can now give the horse the order and cue to raise his leg. As soon as the hoof leaves the ground your assistant keeps it held up and out for a few seconds while you pat and praise your pupil. All this should be done quietly and calmly. Repeat the exercise a few times, seeing that the leg is extended straight in front. Your horse will soon gather what is required.

The next stage is to make him turn. You stand in the position as before, but in your left hand (which holds the off-side rein) you also carry a long stick. Your horse knows the cues for turning on the forehand so he should move his hind quarters away from you as soon as the order is given. But naturally before he is cued for this movement he is made to extend his foreleg, which is then held by the attendant.

Now he has to turn, keeping his foreleg raised and extended all the time. This is difficult, so you must be satisfied with a few paces to start with, and only as long as the horse is willing to keep his leg extended. Your assistant has the job of seeing that this left leg is always lying comfortably in relation to the body; as he holds it he must turn with the hind quarters. If he turns too quickly or too slowly he may hurt the animal or hinder his movements.

Fig. 25 gives a good idea of the exercise, but the hoof should really be placed nearer the centre of the tub.

It stands to reason that if we wish the horse to move in the opposite direction, we must stand on the opposite side of the horse and use the other hand for the various movements and cues.

PUSHING

Your horse carries short bearing reins, and two loose reins are clipped to the snaffle rings. These are pulled over the horse's head and lead straight from either side of the bit to each hand of your assistant, who walks directly in front of the horse and close to him. You, walking at the near side, order him to 'Push!', at the same time using the whip to urge him forward. Directly the assistant — who up till now has been standing — feels the horse's nose on his back he immediately walks on (Fig. 26). He should not wear spurs in case the horse treads on them, and he should be careful that the horse cannot hurt his head on any buttons, buckles, etc. When the horse obeys the order to push, the assistant must walk on slowly so that the horse can easily push him again, but he must move directly he feels the horse's head, for this brings the horse his reward.

26 The first lesson in pushing. My assistant has to move directly he feels the horse's head in the small of his back. (Lijsen with Pitschourikian.)

First lessons in pushing with Mary Chipperfield, who holds a tit-bit to encourage Star to push her back. (David Jamieson)

You then take the assistant's place.

The trick can be presented with loosened bearing reins in which case the horse is better able to give you a good big nudge, or it can be worked with fairly tight bearing reins at a trot.

PIROUETTE

The pirouette, as performed by a Liberty horse, is a complete turn made about his vertical axis, which lies at approximately the position of his surcingle (Fig. 27). After one complete circumgyration he continues on his way; therefore, at the end of a pirouette the horse is in exactly the same position as he was when he started.

27 *Pirouette. This photo was not taken at a very good moment. The horses should always remain parallel. Here each is at a different stage: though the first is nearly half way round, the third has not even started. (A. van Os.)*

The easiest way to train him is to fasten the bearing reins in the usual way, but also clip on a pair of ordinary reins to the snaffle rings and let your assistant ride him.

Starting, as is customary, on the left rein, the cues are as follows:

(a) The forelegs must first leave the ring fence, so in the first lesson you order, 'Come!' as in the call to the centre of the ring, throwing the thong of your whip over to your left and taking one pace backward.

(b) As soon as the horse bears away from the ring fence, take a step forward and throw the thong further to the left, then twice as far to the right.

(c) Next throw the thong again behind the horse from right to left and bring him back to the fence.

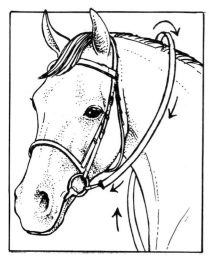

Wrapping the lunge around the neck in preparation for the pirouette.

This is the easier and less cumbersome way. Putting the lunge around the horse's neck in this way helps to guide him round in the training stage.

28 Pollux is ready for his first pirouette lesson. The lunge has been thrown over his neck and brings him inwards. The assistant, holding a short lunge fixed to the inside snaffle ring, shows him the way by following the horse's tail and keeping the lunge taut. (Lijsen with Pollux.)

All we have so far done is to make the horse describe a small circle, but that is enough at the outset.

The rider's first job is to use his near rein and heel to help the horse understand what is required. In the first lessons the movements should be done on the same spot, so as not to confuse the animal.

Next, the rider must try to make the circle smaller and smaller, and now we give the horse the order 'Pirouette!' instead of 'Come!' Apart from this the rider must always be ready to help the horse and correct when necessary. But *only* when necessary.

When the horse seems to understand, try it without the rider. At first you may find that you need your assistant to help the horse by walking level with the horse's tail holding in his inside hand a short lunge, fixed to the inside snaffle ring, with which he can gently pull the head round at the order to pirouette, and passing quickly behind the tail help the horse to complete the turn.

However, I work in a rather different way. I fasten the long lunge to the near-side snaffle ring, the horse still being on the left rein and travelling anti-clockwise round the ring. Then I toss the lunge over the horse's neck and back under his lower jaw, and from here it leads to my hand as I stand near the centre of the ring, slightly in front of the horse so that I can just see his off-side eye.

A second short lunge is fastened to the near-side snaffle ring and leads back to my assistant who walks level with the tail on the near side. At the order to pirouette, the whip cues are given as already described, and the assistant walks round the rump of the horse (Fig. 28). The horse naturally follows the assistant with the short lunge, and in doing so, unwinds the long lunge which must now be wound round the horse's neck again before the next pirouette.

When your horse really understands what is wanted, you can rehearse without an assistant.

Obviously the first lessons are given at the walk. But when you know the horse will obey implicitly you can try the trick at the trot.

You should rehearse it no more than twice on each rein during one lesson to start with; and then always on the same spot. After he gets used to it, it is a good idea to take three or four turns with the lunge round the horse's neck, one for each pirouette you

The lunge line is placed around the neck to aid in early lessons in pirouette. (David Jamieson)

intend the horse to make. Always remember to keep the horse moving. If you have to adjust the lunge after each pirouette it becomes a very slow affair, not worth looking at.

Another worthwhile tip, when you first want the horse to pirouette without the rider, is to make the outside bearing rein longer than that which is nearer to you. But directly the horse will pirouette without any hesitation then keep both bearing reins the same length.

The trainer should stand, as I have already said, so that he can see the horse's off-side eye. The assistant remains as near the horse's tail as possible.

WALTZING

As a matter of fact waltzing is really nothing more than two horses, head to tail, performing a series of pirouettes together. If you would like to include this routine in your act, then proceed as follows:

Let us imagine that your two horses are walking round the ring in Indian file on the left rein. You first order the second horse to change. You will probably find it advisable to have the leading horse ridden for the first few lessons so that he learns to follow the ring fence and *not* obey the order given to the second horse, who is now on the right rein and walking round the ring in the opposite direction. He must always pass the first horse on the inside, and it is the second horse that we must follow with the whip.

Passing each other is taught as a preliminary exercise. The horse on the right rein always passes on the inside of the horse on the left rein.

When you want them to waltz, bring them to a stop along side each other, remove the lunge, and harness them together with a shortish length of cord leading from a ring on the crupper of each to the noseband of the other where it can be clipped in place. It is best to have both horses mounted for the first few lessons, although they must know how to pirouette individually in perfect fashion before you start. At the order, '*Valsez!*' they are made to turn a pirouette round each other.

But they must also move forward. This can be achieved with the help of an assistant who urges them on from the outside of the ring while you remain at the centre giving the cues, as for a pirouette (Fig. 29).

29 Waltzing ponies. (Lijsen with Mammy and Lizzy.)

The tip of the the whip should always point at the horse which is turning inside. If the cords are too short it will hamper the forward movement round the ring. The horses should remain harnessed together until they move perfectly. And that is all there is to it, except for one tip. *Always keep your horses waltzing until they have passed the ring doors.*

Always finish waltzing after passing the doors so as to stop the horses leaving the ring without permission.

See illustration, p. 29.

SITTING

This is merely the getting-up routine, from a lying down position, halted halfway. When your horse is lying down, the order is given to rise. Directly the forehand is up, two assistants place their hands on the croup of the horse and press down, preventing him from raising his hind quarters.

Needless to say with all these tricks, whenever the horse does or even attempts to do what is wanted, he must be rewarded and made much of. In this trick you will find that your horse learns to rise slowly and easily.

KISSING

Stand in front of your horse with a carrot or a piece of bread sticking out of your mouth. It should be as long as possible. Now take hold of the noseband and bring the horse's nose round towards the titbit. Let him take it. When you have done this a few times he will start to look for the titbits in your mouth.

You must teach him to associate this with the order 'Kiss me!' Then you can gradually decrease the reward, until he really does kiss you, but give him a reward from your hand all the same.

Do not do this trick too often in case the horse takes to biting or snapping at your face.

CALCULATING HORSES

What you have to do here is to get your horse to paw the ground with one leg (the near foreleg for preference) at the slightest cue, and to continue until another cue is given for him to stop. Both these cues must be so subtle that the audience will not notice them. This is made easier because the horse, having eyes at the side of his head, can see what is going on slightly to the rear as well as in front.

First, stand at the near side and tap the horse's leg until he starts to paw the ground. As soon as he stops tap him again. You will find that he soon begins to paw when the whip is merely pointed in the direction of his leg. When you move the whip in the direction of the leg, lean forward as if you were bowing. After a little while he should start when you lean slightly forward and stop when you stand upright.

ROUTINES FOR MORE THAN ONE HORSE
CHANGING PLACES

In this routine Number Three takes the place of Number One, Number Four takes the place of Number Two and so on. Since the word 'Change' is very like that used for changing rein — and also because horses are usually spoken to in French — the order generally given is '*Remplacez!*'. The use of the whip is more

This is just one of many different ways of changing places. In this case, horses 3 and 4 move to 1 and 2, and once in place the original 1 and 2 (now 3 and 4) do the same. The horse must know his name and follow the guider.

30 Friesland horses in the neck-over-neck routine. (Lijsen.)

In other words the horses should be moving side by side.

difficult and requires quite a lot of practice. The thong should be thrown over the horse's neck and made to touch the further shoulder. Be careful that it keeps well away from the eyes. Further details are given in the general instructions below.

NECK OVER NECK

In this trick horses stand in line abreast and place their chins over the neck of the horse alongside (Fig. 30). The training is the same as that used in the next trick.

NECK OVER TAIL

Here the horses also stand in line abreast but alternately facing in opposite directions. The same movement is made.

For both these tricks bearing reins are dispensed with. The main thing is to see that a titbit is offered over the neck or the crupper of the next horse, giving him the correct cue so that he associates this with the reward. This can be a stick cue. To start with, hold a stick against the near side of the horse's nose, and get your assistant to offer a lump of sugar across the neck of the next horse. You will soon find that while the horse stands still you have only to raise the stick and the head will go over the neck or crupper in search of a reward.

TWO DEEP

The even-numbered horses should come up on the inside of the odd-numbered ones. The order is 'Two deep!' or 'Par deux!' followed by the name of the second horse. The horse should come out as for changing places, if he does not obey, touch him on the inside shoulder with the whip as you call his name.

ACTS WITH MORE THAN ONE HORSE

The easiest way with a troupe of Liberties is to begin by training them mounted. Fortunately this does not mean that you have as many riders as there are horses, for you will start with no more than two of the troupe in the ring together: first 1 and 2, then 2 and 3, next 3 and 4, and so on.

It is most important that each horse should get to know his name. You must take every opportunity of talking to the horses individually in the stable, calling each by name and giving him a titbit, so that in the end each one will prick his ears at the sound of his name.

When they are in the ring the riders should help as little as possible, waiting until the last minute to prevent a mistake, or correcting it immediately it is made. But they should continue to ride until the horses perform perfectly.

You should start by teaching them to stop, move on, change rein and come to the centre.

You already know that a horse will only do a trick when travelling in the same direction as he was when the trick was taught. For instance, if a horse has been trained to change places on both reins, he will do it whenever the cue is given; but if he has been taught to do this only when travelling anti-clockwise round the ring, no amount of cues, cajolery or anything else will make him do it out of the blue on the other rein. This can be turned to your advantage, for you will find that it saves you a lot of trouble if you teach certain tricks on one rein only.

Performance with a group of Liberty horses. Yasmine Smart with Austen Brothers Circus. (Bob Langrish)

If you want the second horse to change direction, and the first horse alone is mounted, then the second horse must be put on the lunge. This routine is not as easy as it looks, for all the horses should obviously keep up the same speed, and if one slackens or hesitates, the next will turn his head and as like as not jump out of the ring. You will probably devote your attention to the horse which slows down, and this is not necessarily the one that you want to change position; the result is what circus people call 'a salad'. So keep the horses up all the time.

In pirouettes the main thing to remember is that some horses, if they see their way clear, either turn very slowly or not at all! When your horses seem far enough advanced to dispense with riders, you may find it useful to have your assistant walk on the outside of the ring-fence to see that the horse performs the movements correctly and to touch the shoulder of the horse with the whip if he is slow to turn.

FIRST PERFORMANCE

The day will come when, after many months of practising, someone will invite you to show your Liberty act at a gymkhana, pony club or horse show. When this happens you may find the following hints helpful.

First of all you must face the fact that however strange it may seem you are 'an attraction'! Although you are not a 'pro', never lose sight of the fact that people may have paid money — and certainly have taken trouble — to see what you can do. They will not expect miracles. They are easily satisfied — far too easily in fact. But try to do your very best. Don't say, 'I'm only an amateur.' This is no excuse and presupposes your shortcomings. If you can't do it, then don't take it on.

Four points of production play an important part in the presentation of any circus act. These are: (a) music; (b) lighting; (c) costume; (d) tempo.

The music must be carefully selected. A short overture, played fairly quietly, should just give you easy time to enter the ring, bow to the audience and turn to face the ring doors. The music should then change for the entry of the horses as you crack your whip towards the ring doors. Directly the horses are in, the doors are closed. All this is done quickly and neatly — without flurry or fuss.

So much for outline, now for the detail.

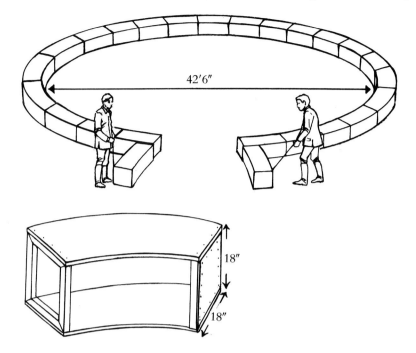

42'6"

18"

18"

A ring fence, showing sectional construction and a manned opening in place of ring doors.

Directly the band strikes up for the overture, you march to the centre of the ring, ring-whip and guider in your right hand. You can wear evening dress with white gloves, but *not* a top hat. Ring-masters and equestrian directors wear top hats at the ring doors, but not while they are working a Liberty number in the ring. At the centre of the ring you stop, place your left foot to the side, draw your right foot to it and click your heels. As you do this you raise the whip and guider, then with your left hand you take hold of the stock below the right hand, turn the whips horizontally and bow over them — not too deeply — to left and to right. Next, taking the guider in the left hand you crack the ring-whip with the right as a cue to the horses to enter the ring.

Your public have come to enjoy themselves, so keep smiling. A smile is one of the greatest assets an artiste can possess — although sometimes it's mighty difficult to keep it up.

As for music, select one of Strauss's waltzes, which the orchestra must play to the rhythm beaten out by the horse's forelegs. They should play with quiet emphasis, but always in time with the horse.

Now about trappings and harness. Whatever is seen in the ring must be spotlessly clean. White is white, not cream. Metal and

Lighting and costume are important parts of the Liberty act. Sacha Houcke of the Circus Barum-Siemoneit at the Monte Carlo Circus Festival. Note that the horse has no harness at all, a more difficult way of performing at Liberty. (David Jamieson)

leather must be polished till they glisten and gleam. Your horse must be groomed till his coat is like silk; mane, forelock and tail must be trimmed.

Never try to show any trick which you are not perfectly sure of, and never try to correct a mistake. If your horse does not change correctly or come when he is called, let him go round again and you repeat the order. If he misses it a second time, order him to stop, go quietly up to him and lead him into the movement you require. In this way you can be sure of a successful outcome, but if you try to correct a mistake directly it is made, the public will immediately notice that something has gone wrong, and it is better to miss a trick out altogether than have that. The public don't usually notice a slip, because they don't know what to expect.

And now for the routine or repertoire.

Your horse should enter on the left rein at a trot. If he is nervous, let him circle the ring three or four times; if he is quiet, make him change after going round once. Then make him change back again after another lap. Halt on the left rein, then on in a trot again. Repeat on the other rein. Change, and then six pirouettes. These should be quick and short as if the horse is waltzing.

Call him towards the centre, not at the dead centre, make him kneel on one knee. While you are doing this, the ring boys should bring in a pedestal which is placed exactly in the middle of the ring. Be careful not to forget that it is there, or you may fall over it.

When your horse has knelt, give him a reward: a small piece of bread is less messy than lumps of sugar. By this time your ring boys should have made their exit. The music, by the way, plays continuously throughout the act.

The horse trots away on the left rein, and you again bring him to the centre and invite him to place his forelegs on the pedestal. You make him move his quarters round the tub once, then, taking a step backward, cue him to step up on the tub altogether. Another circle in this position and you ask him to step down, but directly his forelegs are on the ground you get him to circle once more while his hind legs are still on the tub, as you follow him round.

Now you give him a reward and in so doing you also give your assistants time to clear the ring. Walk your horse to the ring fence, glance at the conductor to tell him to change the music to a minuet or tango and you make your horse circle the ring in a Spanish Walk. You keep level with him about a yard off, lifting your legs in time with his. The conductor must follow the time, however erratic, beaten out by the horse; the animal is the sole source of rhythm. If it sounds odd, remember this is a circus performance, not a concert.

Ask your horse to come to the centre, then make him kneel and lie down. Don't forget to loosen his bearing reins first, if you want him to turn his head. Sit on his flank and give him a piece of bread. While this is going on, two of the ring boys move around the outside of the ring fence, carrying white poles about

Once the horse has learned to lie down correctly, the next step is to pat his flanks prior to sitting lightly on them. See p. 29.

8 ft long. When you are ready, your horse gets up, the ring boys come into the ring and put one end of the poles on the ring fence and hold the other level, for the horse to jump over. Meanwhile the bearing reins have been refixed.

Let your horse go, give the conductor the cue to change to a gallop in 6/8 time. The horse should clear the jumps on each rein, then the ring boys quickly move together at the ring doors and hold the poles at a different height. You let your horse turn straight across the ring and clear both bars and ring fence in a dashing climax. Your assistants leave as quickly as possible. And you stand alone in the ring acknowledging the applause with a series of bows. The ring doors are opened for you, and you make your exit.

1. (opposite) An early exponent of High School riding in the circus, François Baucher at the Cirque Franconi, mid nineteenth century. (G. Margot)

2. *(opposite above) The full meaning of Liberty. Circus Gruss. (David Jamieson)*

3. *(opposite below) Fredy Knie Snr and his Liberty horses. (David Jamieson)*

4. *Mary Chipperfield and Pedro in performance. (David Jamieson)*

5. *(above) Mary Chipperfield and her troupe of Liberty Arabs. (David Jamieson)*

6. *(below) An Edwardian theme in a solo Liberty act by Indian, presented by Mary Chipperfield at the Blackpool Tower Circus. (David Jamieson)*

7. *(opposite above) A platoon in eighteenth-century costume: John Lassetter's Lipizzaners at Goodwood, 1991. (Bob Langrish)*

8. *(opposite below) Colourful quadrille presented by the East Grinstead Riding Club at the Horse of the Year Show. (Bob Langrish)*

9. (opposite above) Royal Canadian
Mounted Police in a carrousel at
Windsor. (Bob Langrish)

10. (opposite below) The Carolis, the
celebrated Italian family of trick riders and
clowns, at the Circus World
Championships. (David Jamieson)

11. A vaulting team at the World
Equestrian Games, Stockholm, 1990.
(Bob Langrish)

12. *The end of the performance. Toulouse-Lautrec, colour crayon, 1899. (Musée d'Albi)*

Part Two

CLASSIC AND CIRCUS HIGH SCHOOL RIDING

INTRODUCTION
SYLVIA STANIER

What does the picture of circus High School conjure up in your mind? To me it means excitement and anticipation, waiting for the curtains to go up, or the ring doors to open, allowing a beautiful horse ridden by a smartly dressed rider to enter.

What is the difference between competition Grand Prix dressage and circus High School dressage? The simple answer is that the circus version is there to please the audience, whereas competition dressage is there to please the judge. The Dressage Committee of the FEI only recognizes certain movements, and lays down strict rules and standards for the compulsory tests. In circus High School all the FEI movements are used, but many extra ones are used as well. For instance, the Spanish Walk is not recognized by the FEI, but what would a circus routine be like without this spectacular movement?

There is perpetual disagreement over what are or are not 'natural' movements. The idea of competition is to prove through the use of only 'natural' movements the suppleness, balance and obedience of the horse. So the purists do it their way and the circus people do it their way. Classical High School dressage can in fact only be achieved through correct basic training.

Lijsen has set out to describe clearly how to teach the horse to perform many interesting movements, and also how to enable the rider to come to the point of performing before an audience. In this part of the book he puts a great deal of emphasis on lateral work.

LATERAL WORK

It seems that many people are confused when dealing with lateral work. In particular, they find it difficult to recognize and distinguish between the various movements. The importance of the lateral movements is immense, as nearly all collected work is brought about by the correct use of lateral movements.

If you watch a performance by the Spanish Riding School of

The Family Knie ready for a circus High School performance. Fredy Knie Snr (left), Geraldine-Katharina and her father Fredy Jnr. (Archiv Knie, Swiss National Circus, Rapperswil, Switzerland)

Vienna, you will notice how they work through shoulder-in and half-pass before proceeding to collected movements such as piaffe, passage and the airs above the ground. It is vital to understand the different lateral movements and the correct order in which they should be attempted.

The place to begin lateral work is, first, with a circle of about 10–15 m diameter, and secondly with a serpentine. The turn on the forehand is also useful in teaching the horse to 'move away' from the rider's leg aid. These exercises are the preliminary ones for the so-called real lateral movements. Once the horse is supple enough to make a reasonable circle and executes a nice serpentine, he should be ready to go on to shoulder-out and leg-yielding.

But what exactly do these phrases mean? What are the movements they describe?

The circle, being round, encourages the horse to begin to bend. The whole idea of lateral work is to supple the horse throughout his frame. The criterion for the correct bend is that the hind legs of the horse follow in the track of the front ones. Once the horse can make a reasonably small (8–10 m) circle, or volte, he is becoming increasingly supple. The circle (like all lateral exercises) can be performed at walk, trot and canter – beginning with the walk. The serpentine is simply a series of half circles, changing the direction and the bend in between each half circle.

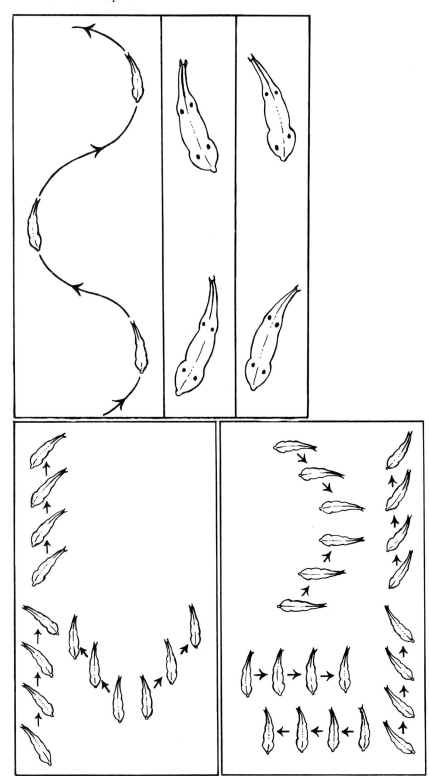

Lateral work (on the left rein) in order of difficulty: serpentine; renvers (top) and travers; shoulder in (top) and shoulder out.

Lateral work: (left) shoulder in, shoulder out, leg yielding in both directions; (right) half pass in both directions, full pass in both directions, travers (top), renvers.

The turn on the forehand is performed from the halt, with the horse pivoting his hind quarters around his forehand. To begin with the horse should only be asked for a quarter turn, which can then be increased to a half turn and finally to a full turn.

The shoulder-out is also asked for with lateral aids, that is, acting leg and hand on the same side. The half-pass, however, is performed with diagonal (or collecting) aids, that is, acting leg and hand on opposite sides. This is more difficult for the horse to perform, so it is introduced at a later stage, when the horse is well used to the lateral aids and supple enough to accept the diagonal aids. It can then go easily into collection.

Shoulder-in is the same as shoulder-out, except — and this is important — in shoulder-out the horse looks at the wall, and in shoulder-in he looks into the centre of the arena.

Leg-yielding is a half-way house before shoulder-out and in. It is most usually performed by making a half-circle on the centre line of the arena, and then with acting lateral leg and hand aids asking the horse to go sideways out of the circle towards the long side of the arena. The horse looks away from the direction in which he is travelling, and the leg off the ground crosses in front of the leg on the ground, with both fore and hind legs.

Leg yielding to right and left on the long rein. Sylvia Stanier with Pedro. (Sylvia Stanier)

Leg-yielding is usually performed on two tracks (see diagram), whereas shoulder-out and in are performed on either three or four tracks. Half-pass, in which the horse looks in the direction he is going, is performed on two tracks.

The half-pass performed on a circle leads into the pirouette at walk and at canter.

The words '*travers*' and '*renvers*' refer to half-pass along the wall, in the first case facing the wall and in the second case facing into the arena. These movements are performed with diagonal aids (unlike the shoulder-out and in) and are thus considerably more difficult.

By skilful use of the volte followed by leg-yielding at trot, *travers* and *renvers* can be introduced quite easily at the beginning of the programme of a display, followed by the more spectacular movements such as passage and Spanish Walk.

NOTES ON THE POSITION OF THE RIDER

As Lijsen mentions (p. 63), he has given an explanation of the rider's seat in another of his works, *Het Ruiterboek*. This is reproduced in full below (from Section VIII, paras. 67–75).

The position of the rider must be quiet and relaxed (no cramped muscles, no forcing of the back). The rider should sit in the deepest part of the saddle (to find this spot, ride a few strides without stirrups). Then allow your seat to slide forward! The top half of the body should be kept vertically in line with the lower leg [i.e. shoulder–hip–heel]. If the lower leg is pushed forwards the top of the body moves backwards; if the lower leg is pushed too far back the body moves forwards.

The shoulders should be squared (not forced) and the rider looks up over the horse's ears (not into his mane). The upper arms hang alongside the body (the rider should feel his coat with the inner part of his upper arm); the elbows do not touch the body, and the lower arm is bent at the elbow.

The hands are held close together above the withers, about 4 to 5 in. apart, and they should stay close, slightly clenched with the wrists turning inwards, and the knuckles parallel. The bridoon reins should be held on the inside. The reins are kept apart on each side of the horse's neck with the little finger or the ring finger. They lie flat on top of one another with the rider's thumbs on top. The stick is usually carried in the right hand (stick, not whip; the whip carries a thong) and there should be slight pressure on the reins.

The rider's legs hang down with the thighs following the saddle-flaps. The knees should also follow the saddle-flaps; the lower leg (calf) should hang down naturally with the heel close to the horse's ribs.

Push the heels out, with the lower leg bent at the knee so that the

This is the easiest place for the hands to be held so as to obtain the best results through the reins to the horse's mouth. The hands are held as close together as is practical for the size and shape of the horse's jaw.

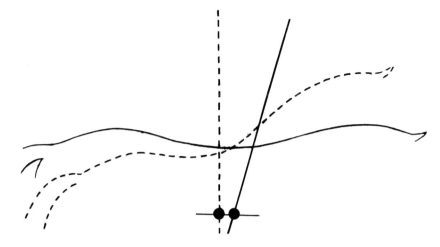

The centre of gravity varies with the position of the horse. The solid line shows the rider's position and centre of gravity on a young or unschooled horse with weight on the forehand, and the dotted line shows the centre of gravity slightly further back with the position of the rider on a schooled horse.

point of the toe is in line with the knee. Vertical lines are (1) hand—knee—toe, (2) shoulder—hip—heel.

The stirrup length is about the length of an outstretched arm, measured from the armpit to the tip of the fingers. With a wide horse they should be a bit shorter than with a narrow horse. Why?

The stirrup should be on the widest part (the ball) of the foot.

The feet point neither completely outwards (dangerous — spurs!) nor completely parallel to the horse. Turn the foot slightly inwards at the ankle. Knees and ankles must be or become supple. (Gymnastics!) Riding a bicycle is a good ankle exercise: put the pedal on the point of the toe and push (this stretches the Achilles tendon).

The rider's centre of gravity should be over that of the horse, so the stirrup should always hang directly over the girth. The horse's speed will increase if the top half of the body is in front of the vertical and decrease if it is behind.

The stirrups are shorter with a wide horse because it is easier for the rider's thighs to encompass the horse and thus keep in balance.

CLASSIC AND CIRCUS HIGH SCHOOL RIDING

Before entering a university one has to pass an examination to show that one has reached a sufficiently high standard of general education to take up more advanced work. Until one's basic schooling is complete, one cannot specialize.

It is the same with horses: though the number of so-called 'School' horses would be very much less if each animal had to pass a test in walking, trotting and cantering correctly along a straight line, while points were deducted for the incorrect movements of the hind quarters and bad head carriage.

Many of the animals one sees move in very strange ways, which still impress the uninitiated although they are completely unnatural. Often the forelegs do all the work; the head carriage is awkward; and the hind quarters, which should always provide the motive power, are trailed along simply because the wretched animal cannot leave them behind. A horse which moves its hind quarters as little as possible — and then not until it is absolutely necessary — will throw its forelegs high in the air in those paces which call for an outstretched limb, such as the Spanish Walk, but the hind legs drag behind drawing lines through the dust . . .

And just as the horse must be well schooled, so should the rider have a thorough knowledge of horsemanship. Not until horse and rider are well versed in all the basic movements of simple dressage should High School work be attempted. The rider should have practised thoroughly and regularly on well-trained horses under a capable instructor.

There are two types of High School. First there is the Classic School, which requires the highest standard of work at the walk, trot and canter, but in which movements requiring the stretching of the forelegs, such as the Spanish Walk, are not allowed as they are considered unnatural. (But work on two tracks cannot be called 'natural' yet this is allowed.) Then there is the Modern School which is that seen in the circus ring where such movements are admitted.

As Lijsen defines this, the Classic School covers the FEI requirements (see glossary), and the Modern or Circus School covers all aspects including Levade, Spanish Walk and many other movements. The Spanish Riding School of Vienna does not recognize the Spanish Walk, nor does the Cadre Noir of Saumur, whereas the Andalusian School in Jerez does. Saumur executes *sauteurs*, but the other two schools do not. Thus the movements included in the classical repertoire vary, but would never be called 'tricks'.

62

Mary Chipperfield and Pedro in a High School performance. (David Jamieson)

The aids and the rider's seat are thoroughly explained in *Het Ruiterboek*, a guide to horsemanship by the present author, but since this has not yet been translated into English it is worth stressing here the first and most important maxim: the rider must be seated in the *centre* of the *deepest* part of the saddle. A perpendicular line dropped from the most forward part of the hands should just graze the front of the knees and meet the tips of the toes (see Fig. 31). A second perpendicular line passes from the shoulder through the hips to the heel.

As the rider always sits well down in the deepest part of the saddle, his pelvis should be at right angles to the horse's backbone. In this way, when riding on a straight line his own vertebrae will run straight up from the centre of the saddle. When turning or circling the horse will incline its body in the direction of the movement, owing to the stronger action of the outside hind leg, and the rider's backbone will also be inclined inwards so that his pelvis remains over the centre of the saddle and at right angles to the horse's backbone.

See pp. 60–1.

31 The alignment of hands, knees and toes.

A rider generally tends to exaggerate his movements in the saddle. What he *should* do is simply distribute his weight according to the horse's movements so that the point of gravity of horse and rider remains as one. THAT IS ALL!

The hands, thumbs on top, remain close together, and the rider endeavours to maintain a correct and quiet carriage of his horse's head.

These rules are basic, and their observation is essential.

If the rider presses his knees down, forcing the weight of his body out of the deepest part of the saddle, his legs become stretched out in front and in this position he will never be able to ride correctly; for, according to the Law of Nature, his weight will tend to work back to the deepest part of the saddle. The leg aids cannot, therefore, be given quietly, because instead of remaining in contact with the horse's body, they swing to and fro. With a rider in this position a horse can never be calm and collected. The aids cannot possibly be given invisibly, as they should be.

We know that the riding whip plays a large part in training, not as a means of punishment but to explain that certain movements, such as stretching or bending the leg, are now required. The trainer must always remain quiet, and he should touch his horse with the whip as little and as lightly as possible. When the desired result has been obtained it is the trainer's *duty* to caress his horse. The trainer who ever forgets this is the kind of man who thinks that training simply consists of punishing mistakes. He could not be more wrong.

Apart from using the whip as little and as lightly as possible, you must see that when it *is* used it is applied at precisely the right time, neither a split second too early nor too late.

Let us suppose that we have taught our horse the Spanish Walk without a rider, as we have described in *Training Horses at Liberty*. We are now ready to make the horse perform this air while mounted. We know that the aid was to tap the leg with the whip as high up as possible. Now we take our time and we do not let the whip continue to touch the horse once the leg is outstretched. In fact, if he has been well trained, you may easily find that the horse will lift his leg directly the whip is held in front of his chest. You need only touch the horse if he fails to stretch his leg.

After a few lessons we must get our horse to move forward

The rider should remain upright in the saddle and use a fairly long, lightweight stick to touch the horse or indicate the command to him. As the horse responds, less and less whip need be used. If the horse does not fully understand the aid an assistant can help.

Spanish Walk in hand in preparation for ridden work.

Mary Chipperfield and Zamora in Spanish Walk ('The March'). (David Jamieson)

and *then* to stretch his leg out high. If we keep on touching the horse with the whip when he is doing what is required, he will get muddled. We touch the horse only to show what he is to do; directly he does it, we praise him and let him know by the tone of our voice that we are well satisfied.

In training you may find it useful to hold a whip in each hand, for then each leg can be touched with the minimum amount of movement.

We may now come to a rather difficult period.

You may feel that the stage in his training has been reached when he should move with a short, springy gait and remain light in the hand; he, on the other hand, wants to stride out. These two conflicting ideas are bound to lead to nervous tension, and your horse will find it difficult to relax.

Of course the curb chain can be shortened (well-known resort of the uninitiated!) but this can only result in increasing the taut sense of conflict. The horse is no longer light in the hand, although a means has been found to *hide* this fact.

At this stage the horse is expected to be working in a double bridle.

What must be done is first to restore the animal's equanimity, the rest will follow.

For training, we should select a horse that is not too young, one of say six years, but who has temperament. Temperament must not be confused with nervous tension; that mistake can cause great difficulties. The horse should be easily managed, and move with a good supple gait. The back of his neck — the line of the mane, as it were — should be a hand or so longer than the front, that is the distance from throat to chest.

Horses descended from trotters are not suitable, nor are race-horses, for they do not as a rule know how to walk, trot or canter, since their speciality is a full extended trot or gallop, and this cannot easily be reduced to a common trot or canter. Mares are difficult, as they become particularly sensitive at certain times of the year. During these periods they do not obey or 'give' to the pressure of the rider's legs, but throw themselves against it with pleasure.

It is wrong to suppose that horses should only be ridden in the school during training periods. Hacking them along roads or across open country at the walk, trot and canter (but nothing more) keeps them fresh and on the bit. Walking on the bit and trotting at a good pace are both extremely beneficial.

Just as the front wheel of a bicycle turns as a result of propulsion coming from the rear wheel, so it is with the horse. The effect of the horse's motive power, which is to be found in his hind quarters, passes along the back and neck and ends in his mouth. We must therefore see that the joints, the back and the neck are kept supple. This is achieved by exercise. First we will deal with the neck.

HEAD CARRIAGE

The highest point of the neck should be between the ears. The nose may occasionally be held vertically, but it must *never* slope down and inwards towards the chest. The horse should remain well on the bit, *eager to go forward* and quicken his pace. He should open and shut his mouth regularly, thus showing that it is supple and sensitive.

BODY CARRIAGE

When a horse is moving in a straight line his body is naturally straight. But when he is moving in a circle his body follows the circumference of that circle, curving around the rider's inside leg. The rider must also automatically form a part of the circle; so that, if he is circling to the right, the left shoulder is slightly in front of the right, and he looks ahead between the ears of his horse.

Most horses used for this work are stallions: they are showy and extremely clever and responsive. Mares are used occasionally, but they can be awkward when in season. Touring groups find it easier to keep to horses of all the same sex.

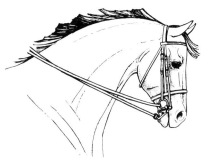

Correct head carriage in a double bridle.

The horse should 'mouth' the bit, i.e. salivate, moving his tongue within a closed mouth.

THE CURB

The curb chain should be flattened *before* being fixed. If this is not done the effect will be painful, as the pressure will be transmitted to the jaw through the one link which is not flattened. The length should be such that two fingers can be inserted between the chain and the jaw. A curb is dangerous in the hands of rough and uninitiated riders, for it works like a lever. It will bring the head down, no matter what position the hands are in. The snaffle has a softer effect and will always work towards the hands. If the snaffle reins run up to the hands they raise the head; if they run down to the hands they lower the head. It is wrong to think that the snaffle always exerts a raising effect.

Here are the exercises which help the carriage of the head and flexibility of the neck.

The rider stands in front of his horse, with the snaffle reins in his left hand and the curb reins in his right in front of the horse's nose. (See Fig. 32.) He brings the nose into the correct position with the snaffle, and then by tugging very gently on both reins he makes his horse open and shut his mouth. This, incidentally, has a most beneficial effect on the ear glands, although its main purpose is to prepare the way for the correct head carriage.

One of the points which should be given particular attention is to see that the horse inclines his head in the right way. For this the rider stands at his horse's side, holding the curb reins in one hand and the outside snaffle rein leading to the far side in the other. By pulling on the snaffle rein he makes his horse turn his head outward while the correct position of the nose is maintained by the hand on the curb reins (Fig. 33). This should be practised in both directions.

You should ask very little of your horse in the early stages. Plenty of patience, many short lessons and lavish praise are the things which produce lasting results.

TRAVERS,* RENVERS† AND PIROUETTE

Your horse trots correctly. That is to say he moves with a lively

---

* *Travers*: nose to wall, hind quarters inside.
† *Renvers*: forehand inside, hind quarters to the wall.

But do not exaggerate these angles. In both *travers* and *renvers* the difference in the distance from the wall of the forehand and the hind quarters should only be equal to the width of the horse's chest so that the outside hind leg steps into the hoofprint of the inside foreleg. (The neck is inclined inwards.) Although moving on two tracks is easier at the trot than at the walk, walking on two tracks should not be neglected. One should remember that in High School the 'inside leg' is always on the side towards which the horse moves, and consequently has nothing to do with the walls of the manège.

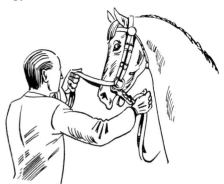

32 *Direct flexion exercise.*

Position of 'ear' or maxillary glands.

This is the method of flexion originally described by the nineteenth-century French horseman François Baucher.

33 *Lateral flexion exercise.*

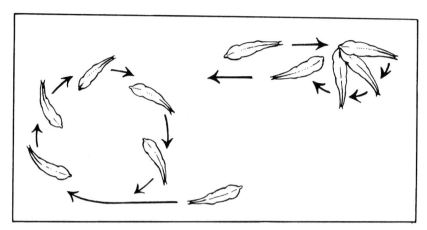

Travers in a circle leading to pirouette.

Many horses have weak or long backs and are thus unable to track up correctly. (See glossary.)

gait, shows suppleness by his outstretched tail and lets his legs come well under his body; as a result of all this he carries his head quietly in the right position; and when we collect him — our legs urging him to make more active use of his hind quarters, while our hands invite him to use the strength developed in an *upward* direction — he moves with shorter, springier steps.

You can now practise *renvers* and *travers* on a straight line, down the wall of the manège. Just before the corner, the horse is put straight again, you then turn on the haunches (see below) and if you have been riding nose-to-wall (*travers*) you return tail-to-wall (*renvers*). You should practise this on both reins, twice in each lesson — not more — with a good interval in between.

As soon as your horse performs these movements correctly you can try riding him in *travers* on the circle. If, very gradually, you make the circle smaller and smaller, you will eventually find him doing a pirouette on the haunches. But remember to be satisfied with a little progress during each lesson. The rider who practises quietly and patiently is bound to get better results; the more slowly you work, the quicker you will get on. But always bear in mind that your aim is a correct and *lively* air. When you are satisfied with these movements performed at the trot, you can practise them at the canter.

The turn on the haunches should first be taught at the walk, and during the first lessons a small half-circle in *travers* is all that should be attempted. This can be gradually narrowed. Under no circumstances should you allow your horse to make the slightest move backward. Directly he attempts this, drive him forward energetically and start all over again.

In equitation the solution to a problem always lies in front, but

Canter pirouette left, executed by Meixner of the Spanish Riding School of Vienna. (R. L. Wätjen, Dressage Riding (J. A. Allen 1958))

the cause generally lies in or behind the saddle.

As soon as your horse is able to show that he can work tail-to-wall and head-to-wall, you should start teaching him to half-pass.

Let us suppose that you are riding round a square. Half-way along one side you turn off, and ride back on two tracks.

Suppose you are on the left rein, you first incline your horse very slightly to the left; but your right calf — *not* your heel, or worse still, your spur — drives the hind quarters to the left so that the off legs pass *in front* of the near legs. After a few lessons, when you arrive on the far side of the track you can continue *on the right rein* tail-to-wall.

Riding on two tracks is really travelling diagonally across the manège while the horse's body remains parallel to the walls on either side. (Imagine a column of men marching to the order 'Right, or left, incline!') The outside calf holds the hind quarters, *the inside calf drives the horse on*, whether in walk, trot or canter. But remember, especially at the outset, that the main movement is *forward*, the sideways movement is always secondary.

In the pirouette, as in every other movement, you should see

The Spanish Riding School in half pass to the right at canter. (Bob Langrish)

A canter pirouette is done in a three or four time canter as near on the spot as possible and is a slow elegant movement. The *tourbillon* is a fast turn on the spot at the gallop, and is not recognised in Classical or circus work.

that your horse's gait remains lively. The horse should remain on the bit even while turning. If you try to accomplish this movement too quickly, you may well find that your horse throws itself round on the inside hind leg while it remains standing on the ground. This is wrong; all legs should be active, the hind legs making a series of steps in a very small circle, while the forelegs describe a circle with a radius little more than the length of the horse's body.

Unfortunately the circus public nowadays has little appreciation of the real art of High School riding, and will often applaud a movement known as the *tourbillon*, or whirlwind, in which the rider makes his horse turn rapidly about his vertical axis. From the point of view of equitation this is of no value whatsoever.

When the half-pass comes quite easily to horse and rider you can try the serpentine movement, which consists of a series of counterchanges or half-passes in alternate directions. If you are on the right rein, for example, you can ride:

3 paces to the right,
6 paces to the left,
6 paces to the right,
3 paces to the left.

You can then make a demi-pirouette and return the same way. It is advisable to insert two steps forward before each change of direction. This makes a more graceful movement.

PIAFFE

This is the state of being collected in its highest form while at the trot; for although the legs are moved in a springy trotting action, the horse remains in one place, marking time, as it were. In no event may the horse move even the slightest bit backward or sideways.

The legs must be raised *slowly* and *high*. The position of the diagonal limbs must at all times bear the correct relation to each other, and the head must be held in the correct position. This means that great attention must be paid to tempo, which must be both regular and slow, to rhythmic movement and to head carriage. I should point out that changes in the diagonal positions are made in the air, so that the near foreleg, for instance, is raised *before* the off foreleg reaches the ground.

You should start by walking your horse on the left rein, holding him with the left hand on the reins under the chin. In your right hand you hold a long stick with which you carefully touch the horse's hind quarters, urging him to move on while your left hand holds him in check.

It is quite probable that your horse will begin to feel uneasy. You must stop at once and caress him until he has calmed down; then start again. Your horse must remain quiet, for if he is not quite calm his movements are bound to become too rapid and consequently fail to reach the height we require.

It is better to let your horse move slightly forward in the early stages of training, otherwise you will find that, although he

Counter change of hand forming serpentine.

This movement is not necessarily taught from the ground, but it is useful to have an assistant whether it is taught from the ground or mounted.

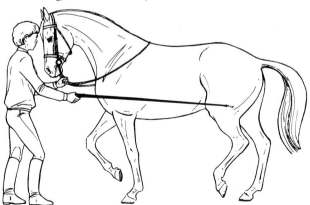

Teaching piaffe from the ground. The whip touches the 'inside' flank, but can also be used higher on the rump if this gives a better response.

moves his hind quarters, his forelegs remain stationary. If you watch some horses, you will notice that one hoof meets the ground before the other is raised. They do not change forelegs in the air. This is far removed from High School, and it is a pity that it is so often seen in circuses.

As soon as your horse understands what is wanted you can begin to touch his forelegs with the stick in order to make him raise them to the proper position. The correct place to touch will have to be found out by trial and error; it may be on the front of the knee or at the back. The forelegs should reach, but not exceed, the horizontal.

Do not keep your horse working too long. One minute of training for the piaffe should be enough for each of the first five lessons. The time can then be increased to two minutes for the next five lessons; and after that you can practise for three minutes at a time. Make it a rule to work the piaffe for no longer than half a minute at a time, however; then walk your horse round and start again at the same spot.

And — *never hurry!*

When your horse has learnt to perform the movements correctly — to raise his legs slowly and high, to bring his hind quarters well under his body and to hold his head properly — you can ask an assistant, who should be as light as possible, to mount. You then make your horse piaffe with a rider on his back, while you stand at his side, touching him with the stick as necessary, and holding the reins under the horse's chin as before.

The assistant sits upright in the saddle, legs close to the horse's body, just behind the girth. All he has to do is to follow the movements of the horse, pressing slightly on the stirrup corresponding to the hind leg that is being lowered, thus lightening the load on the leg that is being raised. That is all. He must, however, sit well down in the deepest part of the saddle. I cannot repeat this too often, for it is one of the golden rules of school riding.

When your horse raises his left hind leg, the rider accepts the movement, thrusting down on the right half of his seat, so as to help the horse; at the same time he presses the horse's side with his right calf thus inviting the horse to raise his right hind leg and left foreleg together. Then, as the right hind leg is raised, the rider thrusts down on the left-hand side, and his calf comes into play. In fact the rider almost piaffes himself, following the

Practising piaffe: Sylvia Stanier and Le Marquis, owned by Princesse H. de la Tour d'Auvergne. (Independent Newspapers Ltd)

movements of the horse's forelegs. But he should remember never to let the toes of his boots come in front of the girth.

Finally, when you have seen from the ground that your horse is working correctly, you can mount and ride him in the piaffe yourself.

Here are the aids: your calves are in light contact with the horse's body *and remain there*, the pressure increasing on the same side and at the same time as the foreleg descends. Your seat, well settled into the saddle, invisibly follows the horse's movements. Your body is upright and your hands are still. If you have to collect your horse, you do this delicately, by turning the little fingers slightly upward towards your body. The pressure is applied to the rein on the side on which the leg is coming down. But there must be no tugging or pulling.

As the piaffe is the acme of collection at the trot, performed on one spot, it is most important to study the section on the passage which follows.

You must also remember that in the piaffe and the passage great attention must be paid to the carriage of the head. If the head is held too low, the horse is not free to move his fore quarters correctly; while if it is held too high it has a bad effect on the hind quarters and back. However, in training, the first thing to do is to see that the horse finds its balance while making the required movements; only when this has been achieved should you try to correct the carriage of the head.

Margaret Chipperfield and Pedro in performance in a very correct and well-balanced piaffe. (David Jamieson)

As we have said before, the hind quarters should come forward well under the body; in this way they carry the weight and leave the forehand free. You can compare this with a wagon in which the load is borne mainly by the rear axle.

Here are some common faults with the aids for correction.

Although the movements are made on the diagonal the horse:

(a) *is too weak in the hind quarters*

Touch the back of the leg that is not sufficiently active with the whip; or, if you have an assistant, get him to put a hobble on this leg, then pull it up and forward as soon as it is raised.

(b) *is too weak in the fore quarters*

Touch the knee that has to be bent, or give an upward tap to the breast and drive the animal forward without increasing the tempo.

(c) *is too quick*

Do not demand more than a few paces at a time but at frequent intervals. If your horse is quiet, caress him; if he becomes uneasy, calm him by talking in a soothing voice, and finish at once.

(d) *tucks his tail in*

This is quite natural and is due to a contraction of the dorsal muscle. It should disappear gradually by itself; unless, of course, it is due to the rider applying the whip too hard.

(e) *puts his legs too close together under the body*

Bring the horse carefully forward, while maintaining the rhythm.

PASSAGE

The movements, positions and aids of the passage are exactly the same as those of the piaffe, the only difference being that the horse moves forward in the state of maximum collection, and, owing to the change of diagonals in the air, produces a very rhythmic pace.

The underlying principle of this air is that the legs of the rider urge the horse to produce more power in the hind quarters, but since this cannot be expended by moving sideways, and the hands hold the forward movement in check, thus regulating the progress, the surplus energy is used in an *upward* thrust, which gives the rhythmic pace, the springiness, which people so often liken to dancing.

It stands to reason that the horse must be perfectly balanced and light in the hand. The curb should only be used in the most exceptional circumstances.

Foreigners call this movement the 'proud air', and they are right, for a horse performing a passage in the correct way looks as proud as a stallion when he sees a mare at the other end of the meadow.

Passage. Member of the Wilmslow and District Riding Club team at the Horse of the Year Show. (Bob Langrish)

The chief difference between the passage of a horse at liberty and a school horse is to be found in the angle at which the nose is carried; in the former it is about 45 degrees while in the latter it is almost vertical, and this naturally has an effect on the length of the paces.

Since a horse performing the passage is in the highest state of collection at the trot, it is obvious that this can only be achieved by degrees. Work on two tracks and similar airs will develop an elasticity, which, in turn, produces a regular, springy trot; but it cannot provide that special rhythmic quality which is so necessary. All now depends on the skill of the rider, and the aids he gives with legs and hands. His legs must work in complete harmony with the diagonal movement of the horse. They must sense, as it were, the power and the function of the horse's haunches and how this is transmitted through the back to the neck and the carriage of the head, and to the forehand and the forelegs.

The easiest way to start training a horse to perform the passage at the trot is to urge the horse forward with the leg aids, while holding him back in as high a state of collection as possible. Directly we find that he has made two or three short, springy paces in perfect rhythm — in other words, that his trot has cadence — we are satisfied, pet him and ride forward at a lively trot. This is the correct way to start — but remember, the rider must have true feeling and the horse must be really supple.

When this cadence has been obtained — and not before — you must pay attention to the carriage of the head. The correct position is a result of accentuated aids from the legs and on the snaffle rein, while more pressure is exerted in the stirrup on the same side as the descending foreleg.

The lessons will then build up as follows: First, correct diagonal, collected trot with correct head carriage. Secondly, correct diagonal, very collected, well-cadenced trot. Thirdly, correct diagonal, very collected, well-cadenced trot with correct head carriage.

It is very difficult for a horse to do the passage from a piaffe (after all, he has been deliberately taught *not* to move forward in the piaffe) but it can be achieved with patience.

If your horse tends to get nervous while learning the piaffe or the passage, cut down the duration of the lessons but increase the number, occasionally letting a day pass without practising this air.

You can stimulate his interest by practising the passage on the way to the stable. If you ride in a school, open the doors and ride round and out, performing this air.

Some time ago a horse was sent to me for correction. He had been trained for High School by a system which is, unfortunately, only too frequently applied. He had been made to do the Spanish Walk for ten minutes at a stretch and to piaffe for twenty minutes without stopping. Not a word of praise did that poor horse receive. Consequently he was very nervous; his tail was never still, and his piaffe consisted of short, jerky little movements.

High School had been started before the horse could either canter, trot or even walk correctly. So I ignored all High School training until the horse became quiet and relaxed once more. Then I rode a half-pass at a collected trot and a few paces at the passage. Then I stopped and was lavish with my praise.

The horse had regained confidence and that was the first essential step towards good training. Fig. 34 shows this horse performing the passage during the time I was correcting the results of his bad training. He had not yet learnt to use his back correctly, and this affects the carriage of his head, throwing the nose in the air. *When the back is used correctly the nose falls. A high back leads to a low neck and a low back to a high neck.*

34 At this stage of his corrective training Favori begins to show improvement. He comes forward and shows keenness but he is not yet supple enough and so the head carriage leaves much to be desired. (Lijsen with Favori.)

COUNTERLEAD

This section serves as an introduction to that which follows. The change of legs at the canter should really be superfluous. Any horse that is destined to be a School horse should have had this drummed into him at an earlier period of his training. As, however, it is most important to appreciate the detail involved it is worth repeating here.

The counterlead must be practised thoroughly on both reins before proceeding to more complicated forms of changing legs. You should start by striking off in counterlead on both reins, then circles in counterlead and so on. Your horse must be quiet, especially at the canter, when his pace must be short and regular. The pace can best be shortened by striking off at frequent intervals. It will not be brought about by cantering for long stretches.

As soon as the canter becomes irregular, your hands should allow your horse to take a little longer pace for a spell. But when he is quiet and composed, you must collect him again — first legs, then hands — and start afresh.

The change of legs should be superfluous because the horse should be so obedient at counter canter (which in this context is the same as counterlead) that he goes on *either* lead in both directions.

35 Counterlead in a canter to the left. The diagonal has been established and now the right foreleg comes forward. (Lijsen with Favori.)

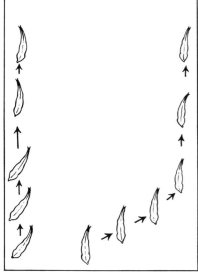

Counter canter through renvers (left) and half pass.

A horse's angle of inclination is related to direction (when circling on the left rein, his body is slightly inclined to the left) and the rider should always look past the horse's eye on the inclined side, pressing down slightly into the stirrup on that side too. In the counterlead, in which a volt to the right is made during a canter on the left rein, the rider should still look past the left eye of the horse although the volt is to the right (Fig. 35).

Do not forget that although you have to describe a circle to the right, your horse throws his weight from the right hind leg on to the left foreleg, for he is in counterlead. This is the result of training. One can see the difference between a trained and an untrained horse when they come to the corner of the school. The untrained horse will lead with its wrong leg and may fall, for it has not learnt to find its balance.

The counterlead greatly helps one to obtain shorter paces at the canter.

But always remember to sit well down in the saddle and to remain still.

If your horse does not understand what is required, then go back to riding *renvers* on both reins and make him strike off in a counterlead and back to a straight line along one of the sides of the manège. Another good exercise is to half-pass at the canter so that the horse comes on to the other rein, then continue your way in a counterlead.

CHANGE OF LEG AT THE CANTER

Your horse has by now been well prepared; you have practised the canter and counterlead *to perfection*, and you know which canter he prefers.

Every horse has a favourite canter, due to the fact that it comes more easily than the other. This may be accounted for by, say, the outside hind leg being a little weaker than the other (it is the strength of this leg which becomes apparent in your horse's angle of inclination), or it may be due to the inside hind leg being stiff and less easily bent. There are many possible reasons.

Let us suppose that he prefers to canter on the left rein. You should then start him off at a canter on the right rein, pass along the diagonal and on arriving at the track on the left rein you ask him to change. This should offer little difficulty and it teaches the horse to understand what is meant. After a few lessons you can start on the other rein, i.e. canter on the left rein, change diagonally and change legs on coming onto the right rein.

As many horses become rather nervous at the beginning of training, always remain as quiet as possible and be lavish with your praise.

You can then start making the diagonal run to the centre of the school. Turn, change and ride back to the track, and there change again. Gradually you can shorten the diagonal line, until you find that you need only ride a few paces away from the wall and then change, ride back to wall, change, and so continue round the school.

Now you can begin working on a straight line. Start off at a canter, ride two paces at the trot, change, canter, and so on. Soon you will find that the intermediary paces at the trot can be omitted and the change made from one canter to the other. When this is achieved try it at every eight paces, gradually reducing this to two paces on each rein.

Next try it on a circle. When you can ride in a circle, eight yards in diameter, at the canter, changing every two paces, your goal is in sight, and you can start changing at every pace. But start by introducing it just at the end of a lesson in which he has shown that he can change at every second pace smoothly and well. Do not ask him to do it more than twice, then praise him and trot away and be satisfied! Changing at every pace makes most horses nervous at the outset and therefore it would be a great pity to make him go on too long.

It is essential to know exactly how a horse canters. The canter consists of five phases. In the first phase his weight is carried by the outside hind leg. This is the left or near hind leg when your horse is on the right rein. The other three legs are in the air, the hooves under the horse's belly. It is therefore the outside hind leg which produces the propulsion. In the second phase the outside diagonal comes into position, which is the inside hind leg and the outside foreleg. In the third phase the outside hind leg, which took the weight in phase one, is now behind the horse and the inside foreleg (on the diagonal) is stretched out in front, leaving the inside hind leg and outside foreleg to meet the ground close together under the horse's belly.

In the fourth phase the inside foreleg reaches the ground, and, in the fifth phase, takes the weight while all three other legs are in the air; the outside foreleg and inside hind leg having just left the ground and the outside hind leg just coming forward, ready

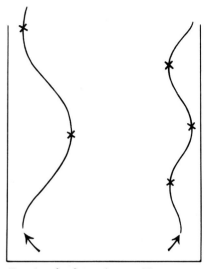

Exercises for flying change of leg, making the distance from the wall smaller and changing at 'x'.

for the first phase again. But before this happens the horse for a short period actually swings on the inside foreleg without the hooves of any of the other three legs touching the ground.

The point at which a change is made occurs at phase five. If the canter is to remain unchanged the outside hind leg comes forward to take the weight (phase I), but if a change is to be made it is the *inside* hind leg which comes forward to open the canter on the other rein.

When changing from a canter with the left leg leading to a canter with the right leg leading, your horse has to start the new canter with the left hind leg, which has to come as far in front of the right hind leg as it was behind it in the previous canter. It is for this reason that the horse must be well collected and the paces kept short, otherwise the distance he has to move his hind leg in changing becomes too great.

All changes must be made smoothly, the horse remaining straight and carrying his head well. The pace which effects the change must always be made in the same way *so that rhythm is maintained*.

The aids for changing are difficult to describe, as the rider's 'feel' of his horse plays such a very big part.

When, in 1870, Germany declared war on France, a number of cavalry officers were required at very short notice. There was no time to teach riding in the orthodox way, so officers were set up on their horses' backs and told to take up the position which seemed to be required by the horse. They were also told to try and follow the horses' movements as if they were making the movements themselves. A lot can be learnt from this lesson.

When we start to walk from a standing position our body is brought forward as a preliminary movement to taking the first step. The rider brings his body forward to start or accelerate a certain air. To stop or slacken pace the body is brought back, which throws more weight on the horse's hind quarters, just as the horse himself throws his weight back when he wants to stop. In the canter to the left our left leg is leading and our right leg follows. On horseback it is the rider's left calf that lies on the girth in a canter to the left, the right calf lies behind it.

And now let us describe the aids for the change of canter. Let us suppose that we are cantering to the left and want to change to a canter to the right. To start with, our horse is throwing his weight from his outside (right) hind leg onto its inside (left)

Flying change of leg at canter.

foreleg, our left calf is on the girth and our right calf behind it. For the canter to the right these positions must be reversed. The moment to change comes when we feel the horse swinging onto its inside foreleg. So, as the foreleg descends, the collection is increased and the position of the calves is reversed, the left calf moves backward behind the girth and the right calf moves forward. At the moment the foreleg meets ground, the left calf, now behind the girth, exerts pressure to persuade the horse to bring the left hind leg forward; for it is this leg which opens the canter to the right. The collection achieved by the hands must be very delicate and should be held only until the hind leg has been brought forward and placed on the ground. Directly this happens the hands relax a little, allowing the other legs to do their share. The rider remains firmly seated in the deepest part of the saddle and on no account stands in the stirrups. No unnecessary moves should be made, and you should make it a rule never to ask your horse to change when he is nervous.

Having once learned the change, many horses will take the initiative and change when they feel like it without any reference to the rider. When a horse changes without being asked, the rider must remain calm and drive his horse on without asking for a change.

Expertise in training is very important here, to prevent the horse from anticipating and to keep him on the correct leg.

36 Spanish Walk on the long reins. (The famous Wittekind.)

THE SPANISH WALK

In the Spanish Walk your horse must perform a lively march with outstretched forelegs, carrying his head correctly all the time (Fig. 36).

The hind leg on a diagonal should be very active, bringing the body boldly forward, and the forelegs are lifted as high as possible while still *remaining in harmony with the hind leg on the diagonal*. In circuses, where it is becoming increasingly difficult to find good School riders, the audience seems to concentrate too much on the foreleg. These are raised higher than the hind leg dictates, and as a result the horse throws his nose in the air, develops a sore back and the hind legs no longer provide the means of propulsion but trail along behind, drawing lines in the sawdust.

The Spanish Walk is actually a Liberty number performed with a mounted horse. It does not form a part of the classic High School repertoire, but that is no reason why it should not be done correctly.

There are various ways of teaching a horse this air, which the reader will find described in *Training Horses at Liberty*. Here is a synopsis.

First your horse must have hobbles strapped round its forelegs. These should be felt-lined leather, the felt protecting the horse from the fastening which holds a ring at the middle of the hobble. This goes to the front of the leg while the buckle and straps go to the back. A short cord is fastened to each ring and held by an assistant. If only one assistant is available then you must practise one leg at a time. Your horse is on the left rein, and you stand on his near side holding him by the reins under the

Hobbles can be used to encourage the horse to raise a particular foreleg. The alternative and somewhat easier way is to touch the horse with a stick at a point between his shoulder and his fetlock until he decides to pick up his leg.

chin. You then tap your horse high up on the leg with a stick held in the right hand. When he takes his hoof off the ground, your assistant raises the leg by means of the cord, trying to get it as near horizontal as possible. On no account must he pull the hoof off the ground, *he must wait until the horse makes the first move*. Directly this happens praise your horse lavishly, but keep the stick in contact with his leg. Only when you move the stick away should the assistant let the leg drop back to the ground.

Your horse will soon learn what is expected of him and directly he stretches out his leg at the correct cue you must then drive him on so that he takes a pace forward as the leg descends. You must see that he takes a long step, otherwise the outstretched leg has no room to remain extended and so bends as it is lowered.

When both legs are moved correctly directly they are touched with the stick, you can dispense with the hobbles, and you try a few consecutive paces.

In Fig. 24 you can see the author touching the horse's leg at its highest point. The stick is kept there until the leg is sufficiently high and the horse is driven on in a lively pace.

See p. 40.

Next the horse is mounted, but you must remain by his side, in order to give the correct aids with the stick. At the same time the rider must give the aids on horseback. These are as follows. First he collects the horse — legs followed by hands — then he presses the calf opposite the horse's leg which you want raised. This brings the hind leg on the side pressed under the body; it is on this diagonal that the foreleg is to be stretched. *The horse must remain well on the bit* and walk with a lively gait.

The rider must remain seated well down in the saddle. He must not slide from side to side, as one too often sees. Furthermore his legs should not move forward and backward. The calves remain stationary, exerting pressure only when required. The horse's head remains straight.

In order to keep the horse on a straight line, while riding along the walls of the school, it is advisable to start off by asking your horse to raise the outside leg. Should your horse raise the wrong leg by mistake, then speak to him in a reproving tone of voice, make him walk on at a lively gait and start again. *Never get flustered*.

Now you can pay attention to the hind legs. They should be touched lightly with the stick at the back of the cannon. This will make the hind quarters more active and produce a livelier gait.

When you have thoroughly schooled your horse from the ground, you can mount him yourself.

All too often does one see a rider whose movements would lead one to suppose that it is he who is doing the Spanish Walk and not the horse at all. His legs fly from hind quarter to forehand, his body swings from side to side and his hands yank continuously at the reins. Not only is this awful to look at, but it

Spanish Walk by High School rider in the circus ring, depicted by Toulouse-Lautrec. Colour crayon, 1899. (Musée d'Albi)

could not be more wrong. So let us list the rules once more:

1. Sit well down in the deepest part of the saddle; the pelvis should be at right angles to the horse's backbone, and your own backbone should be vertical.

2. Legs held close to the horse's body, so that pressure can be given with the minimum effort. The leg which is not exerting pressure remains behind the girth. If you want your horse to raise its right leg, you will apply pressure through your left leg and lightly on the right rein, and vice versa.

3. The hands remain close together, thumbs uppermost. You collect your horse and when you want him to raise a leg you turn the hand so that the little finger moves in towards the body. When, however, the leg has reached the highest point, the collection is gradually relaxed for your horse has to make a long stride. If you do not let your horse advance, the foreleg will bend as it is lowered and you will lose the harmony of the movement on the diagonal, the corresponding hind leg cannot work correctly and the gait becomes irregular.

THE SPANISH TROT

As the name implies this is the same movement performed at the trot. Once again you must remember three things: a correct trot, a correct position of the outstretched leg and the correct carriage of the head. If one of these is not as it should be, you cannot say that you are performing the Spanish Trot. Many people *think* that they are making their horse do a Spanish Trot when, in spite of a high foreleg, the horse's nose is high up in the air and the trot is incorrectly made. All this will lead to is a sore back.

The public, who so often only look at the forelegs — if they looked further many a School rider would be out of work — applaud vociferously and think the rider wonderful; but those who *know*, merely pity the poor horse.

Yet this is not a difficult air to teach. If your horse has temperament, all you have to do is to teach him the Spanish Walk and urge him to go quicker and quicker. This time you should be riding and your assistant walks at the side of your horse. He must watch very carefully and if, when you start trotting, the horse fails to extend his foreleg, then he must tap it just as you did when training your horse to do the Spanish Walk. After a few paces at the trot stop and caress him, and he will soon realize exactly what is wanted.

Let the horse take long strides, as in the Spanish Walk; move your hands as little as possible and remain as still as you can in the saddle. Try to give all aids invisibly. Those given by the legs are the same as in the Spanish Walk, but follow more quickly to fit the tempo of the trot.

Should your horse show little temperament or appear slow you may have to try another way. This is to walk your horse on the left rein while you walk beside him, just as if you were teaching him the Spanish Walk. But your assistant also holds a whip and urges him to trot, while you see that he extends his forelegs. As soon as he understands, mount and proceed as outlined above. If no assistant is available you must ride your horse at a collected trot and touch the forelegs with your whip as in the Spanish Walk.

POLKA

You may well find it difficult to teach the polka to a horse that already has learnt the Spanish Walk because he has been drilled to extend each leg at every pace in the Spanish Walk but for the polka he is required to raise it only after every third step. As we have already explained in *Training Horses at Liberty*, a horse does not automatically perform on one rein an air which has been learnt on the other. Many a School rider profits by this, performing the Spanish Walk on one rein and the polka on the other.

The best method is first make your horse raise his leg and then urge him on quickly in an ordinary walk. In this way you can teach him that he is *not* required to raise his foreleg at every pace. Once this has been established in the horse's mind you can give him the cue to raise his leg at decreasing intervals until he only takes two ordinary paces *between* the end of one extended step and the beginning of the next extended step. You must of course see that the horse goes forward in a lively fashion as the out-stretched leg comes down. This is the great difference between polka and the Spanish Walk, for in the latter the horse remains collected, and the aids given by the leg are continuously applied.

Once the walk has been mastered you can try it at the trot, and since the polka is a lively dance, you will find that it is at the trot that it looks its best.

KNEELING AND OBEISANCE

Since this is really a routine which belongs to the Liberty act (Fig. 37) the authors would refer you to *Training Horses at Liberty*.

37 Europe's best horsewoman demonstrates the obeisance. (Madame Lungen with Maestoso.)

NOTES ON AUXILIARY REINS

1 The running martingale

The effect of the martingale is to bend the neck. It lowers the head that is held too high. The snaffle reins should pass through the rings of the martingale, not the curb reins as these would cause pain when the horse threw his head up. It stands to reason that once the horse has lowered his head to the correct position, the martingale should no longer exert a downward pull. It must therefore be quite loose when the head is in the right position, and the snaffle reins should run through the rings *straight* from the bit to the rider's hands. When used in conjunction with a thick snaffle bit a martingale has a soft effect on the corners of the mouth, and the added advantage that the reins lead to the mouth at the correct angle even if the rider holds his hands too high.

2 The standing martingale

To some extent this rein, which leads from the girth upward, has the same effect as a martingale. But since it is fixed by a buckle to the back of the noseband and has no rings for the reins to pass through, it makes it impossible for the horse to throw his head up.

The great difference, however, is that with a martingale, if the snaffle reins lead directly up to the hands, they can invite − often unconsciously − the horse to hold his head higher, which a standing martingale renders impossible. Therefore the standing martingale may remove a bad effect, but *it does not correct the cause.*

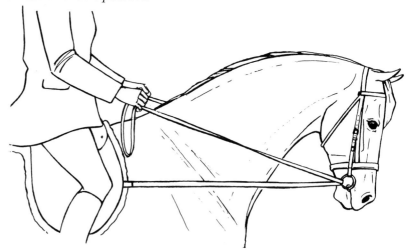

Ordinary running reins from the saddle to the hand.

A distinction should be made between running reins, which attach to the D-rings of the saddle or the girth straps, and draw reins which run between the horse's legs and attach to the girth under the belly.

3 Running reins

These sliding reins lead from the D-ring at the side of the saddle through the snaffle rings, from inside outwards, and back to the hands. In order to ensure that the reins run easily through the snaffle rings, the smooth side of the leather is placed in contact with the metal. The effect is that of a purchase, or what in the Navy they call a 'runner'. The power gained is double; it is therefore a harsh devise if put in inexperienced hands. As experience can only be gained by practical trial, it is a hard school — for the horse! By understanding the theory, however, you will not only learn quicker but save your horse as well. The great thing to remember is that as the power gained is twice, your horse will appear twice as light when on the bit. The danger lies in forgetting this, so that when the horse gives, instead of letting the hands remain quiet, the rider shortens the reins until he feels in contact with the animal's mouth once more. Consequently the horse's nose is brought down and in, resulting in bad head carriage, and the lively gait — always the first requirement — is utterly lost.

But I have adapted the principle of the running rein, and designed a rein which suits everyone, from experienced horseman to novice. The reins are divided, quite naturally, into two equal lengths, one for each side. But each rein is again divided into two parts of unequal lengths. Let us call these 'A' and 'B'. Part 'A' is 16 in. long and has a swivel clip at one end, a buckle at the other. Part 'B' is 72 in. long, and for the first 24 in. it is punched with holes to fit the prong of the buckle at the end of part 'A'. At the point where these holes come to an end there is a metal bar, set at right angles to the rein, and extending a sufficient length on

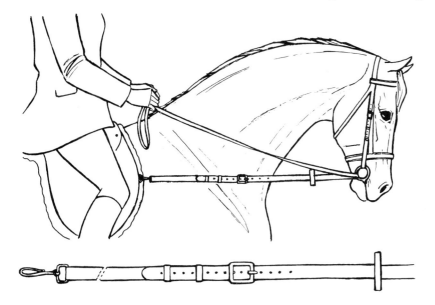

Lijsen's adapted running rein, showing the position of the two straps and the metal bar.

either side so that it cannot slip through the snaffle ring. The remaining 48 in. of rein is quite plain. It can eventually be buckled to the remaining 48 in. of the similar rein on the other side.

The short length 'A' is clipped to the saddle and the buckle end, for the moment, is left hanging down. The long length of plain rein 'B' is threaded through the snaffle ring from the inside outwards until it is prevented from going further by the bar. This leaves the punched end hanging down inside the snaffle ring. This end is then fastened to the buckle of rein 'A' at the correct distance so that the horse's head is carried in the correct position when the metal bar meets the inside of the snaffle ring.

The result of this device is that when the horse throws his head up or pulls hard, the effect of the purchase comes into play, *until the head assumes the correct position*. At this point the bars come into contact with the snaffle rings and the rein works in the ordinary way, the return length, running from bar to saddle, lying loose until the horse, by throwing his head up or stretching his nose out, once more takes up the slack.

Anyone can use this adaptation without the slightest risk.

4 Side reins

Although side reins have been used for centuries, and have un-doubtedly led to excellent results, I feel one must — however reluctantly — closely examine their use and effect.

Although in training Liberty horses their purpose is different, in equitation the function of the side rein is to ensure the correct carriage of the head while being lunged and, by making the hind quarters more active, the horse brings his hind legs further under the body, which causes a rise in the fore quarters and a drop of the head. This is plain enough, but I want to draw your attention to two objections, which, although they may not be immediately evident, are none the less always present.

Objection 1: We want the horse to *raise the forehand gradually, and*, as a result, *to adopt the correct head carriage*. At the same time we want him to learn to give. He must therefore develop a flexible and supple neck, particularly just behind the ears, and start nibbling at the bit. Consequently the training plan *should* run as follows:

First, the horse extends his nose and neck and then raises the forehand. Next, he gives to the bit and gradually lowers his nose.

But how do side reins work in practice?

The horse tries to extend neck and nose, but is able to achieve this only within the limits of the reins, so the neck is never completely free.

Then, because withers and mouth are connected by the side reins, one might logically expect a lowering of the nose and a development of giving.

But on close examination things do not turn out quite as one might expect. A glance at Liberty, jockey and pad acts in the circus will show you that too often horses avoid giving by stiffening the neck and dropping the head too far, the nose coming behind the vertical. They do not flex the neck behind the ears but bend it near the withers, the fixed point of the side rein. And they are very apt to get behind the hand.

Objection 2: When side reins of equal length are fastened to the side of the withers, the most illogical effect comes into play when the horse travels in a circle. The horse feels the *outside* rein, not the inside one, which, instead of being tight, now hangs loose!

It is the weight and pull of the lunge which brings the horse's head in, helped by the action of the outside hind leg. The best thing you can do is to let the horse find out the correct inclination for himself, and not to obstruct this by fixing side reins of equal lengths to the withers. Of course you can shorten the inside rein,

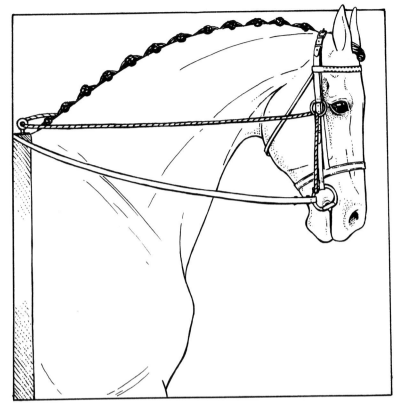

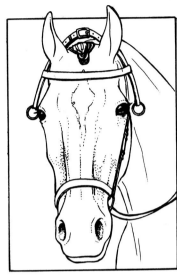

*Lijsen's adapted bearing rein.
This is not a recommended piece of
equipment today.*

but much the best solution is to have a side rein in the form of a cord running freely from one side of the bit, through a pulley clipped to the centre of the girth on the withers, round to the other side of the bit. Such a side rein allows a horse to move its head to either side. It should not be too tight at the start, but applied gradually, as if it led not to a fixed pulley but to a rider's hand.

But should one use side reins at all? Because to me they seem quite illogical, I prefer to use a different method. During the first lessons I use a rein which is similar to the bearing rein used in training carriage horses, with the difference, however, that my rein is fixed near the withers, above the normal position for a bearing rein. Two short straps each carry a ring; the other end is punched with holes in one case and carries a buckle in the other. These ends are pushed up through the slots of the brow-band and buckled together between the ears, the rings being level with the horse's eyes. For a rein I use a length of cord which I tie to one snaffle ring and lead up through the ring at eye level down to a pulley fixed to the top of the girth, then up to the ring at the other eye and down to the other snaffle ring. This rein should *follow* the raising of the head, but once the horse has raised his head it tends to persuade him to keep it there, though he can still move his nose forward and his head from side to side.

Not until the horse realizes how the forehand should be raised (by means of this raising rein) should any attempt be made to teach the correct carriage of the head. Then a lower rein can be fixed nearer the position of an ordinary side rein.

If later, you use curb and snaffle, you can fix side reins — not too tight — to the curb.

The idea of taking side reins up to the top of the withers, instead of half-way down the horse's side, may strike some people as odd. But I can assure readers that the results more than justify a trial. This is the natural position for the hands. So the direction of effort resembles that of the ideal rider, one whose hands are never out of place.

FIRST PERFORMANCE

Here is a repertoire which, with practice, you should now be able to present (Fig. 38):

1. Enter at a lively trot, hat in hand, to music played in 2/4 time.
2. Volte.
3. Serpentine.
4. *Travers*, demi-pirouette, *renvers*, half-pass, *renvers*.
5. Counterchanges.
6. Passage to the centre to music at a slower tempo.
7. Piaffe.
8. Spanish Walk to a tango or a minuet.
9. Spanish Trot to a polka.
10. Canter to a tune in 6/8 time.
11. Volte.
12. *Travers*, *renvers*, half-pass.
13. Demi-pirouette.
14. Counterlead, volte.
15. Canter with a change at every eight paces, twice; every four paces, four times; every two paces, eight times.
16. Canter to centre and pirouette.
17. Kneel.
18. Passage, hat in hand, to exit.

The rein can be attached to the curb bit, but only to improve an already excellent collection and balance of the horse — in other words, on a very highly schooled horse in the hands of an expert.

38 Waiting to enter the ring. This shows you the correct dress for a man; if you are a woman nothing looks better than a habit — see Fig. 37. (Lijsen with Favori.)

The end of the performance. Margaret Chipperfield and Pedro. (David Jamieson)

Part Three

MOUNTED QUADRILLES, CARROUSELS AND OTHER EQUESTRIAN MANŒUVRES

INTRODUCTION
SYLVIA STANIER

'Carrousel' is a word rarely used today, so it is worth a few sentences to describe what it means. From the time of the Renaissance until the mid nineteenth century — and to a smaller degree until the period just before the First World War — the French notables gathered at musical equestrian galas to enjoy themselves and show off. For instance, during the reign of Louis XIV (the Sun King) galas were held in which carriages as well as ridden horses were paraded. These gatherings were held in the Royal Riding School at Versailles and were, to say the least, grand and spectacular. Pageantry was one of the main priorities. However, particularly as time went on, certain patterns and particular routines were drawn up especially for the High School work and were strictly adhered to. These came to be known as carrousels.

During the nineteenth century the famous L'Etrier Club in Paris was a meeting place for enthusiastic equestrians. Membership was much sought after and much prized when obtained. One of

Louis XIV dressed for the carrousel. Engraving by Chaveau, 1670. (Courtesy of Sylvia Loch)

94

the rules was that at each year's annual gathering each member had to ride a new horse in a new routine containing different movements to those used the previous year. The standard was extremely high. The best trainers, the best costumiers — in fact, the best of everything — were used.

Thus 'carrousel' is an old but much revered word. Today we more usually use the term 'quadrille', and the best-known examples of quadrilles are those so successfully performed by the many Riding Clubs who try to qualify for the Horse of the Year Show in England and, on the Continent, for their own championships — the successors to the L'Etrier galas and the Versailles revelries.

Lijsen's work has a lot to offer in this field, because it contains many of the routines and patterns still in use today, and many tips and ideas which may be useful to people thinking of joining their local Riding Club's quadrille team or forming one themselves.

Quadrille in an indoor riding school of the early-eighteenth-century type.

MOUNTED QUADRILLES, CARROUSELS AND OTHER EQUESTRIAN MANŒUVRES

The metric equivalent of these measurements is 25–30 m long and 12–18 m wide. However, the standard dressage arena is 40 m long (or 60 m for FEI competition) and 20 m wide, and these are the dimensions which would normally be used.

A manœuvre consists of riding in formation and taking part in a series of evolutions, which, when completed, make a whole. It is something like an equestrian square dance, and is often referred to as a Musical Ride. The manège, riding-school or arena in which it is performed is usually twice as long as it is broad. A length of 80 to 100 ft and a width of 40 to 58 ft are average dimensions. Many movements, however, can be performed in a circus ring with the standard diameter of 42 ft.

'Platoon' of riders from the Spanish Riding School. (Bob Langrish)

It is advisable to choose quiet, well-trained horses, which will behave themselves when ridden close behind or at the side of others. An even tempo must be maintained throughout. If one group is found to lag behind, the riders should not increase the pace in an effort to catch the others; rather they should cut the corners, while those ahead should slow down until the lost ground is made up.

The total number of people taking part should be divisible by the number of groups required by the various movements. Let us take, as an example, twelve riders, six ladies and six gentlemen. These are divided basically into two platoons: the first consists of the ladies, the second is made up of the gentlemen. Each platoon is then divided into two sections, in this case, of three riders each. Ladies riding side-saddle should always be stationed to the left of the gentlemen; if riding astride they take up their position to the right. In either case the ladies' platoon is the leading platoon. A plan of the company would look like this, if the ladies rode astride:

GENTLEMEN'S PLATOON	LADIES' PLATOON
1st Gentleman	1st Lady
(*Leader of 2nd Platoon*	(*Leader of 1st Platoon*
and of the 1st Section	*and of the 1st Section*
of the 2nd Platoon)	*of the 1st Platoon*)
2nd Gentleman	2nd Lady
3rd Gentleman	3rd Lady
4th Gentleman	4th Lady
(*Leader of 2nd Section*	(*Leader of 2nd Section*
of the 2nd Platoon)	*of the 1st Platoon*)
5th Gentleman	5th Lady
6th Gentleman	6th Lady

Great attention should be paid to the method of giving commands. Most commands should consist of two distinct parts: the first is preparatory, the second is executive. There should be a pause between them. For instance, in the command, 'Large circle ... Ride!' enough time must be allowed between the preparatory description and the executive order to enable the riders to get ready. In cases where the place at which the movement is to be made is given in the command, no executive order is needed. 'Form a large circle, in the centre,' makes it sufficiently clear that the company will follow the leader, who will obviously leave the track when he gets half-way along one side. Similarly, 'Change rein, along the diagonal,' means that the riders must follow the diagonal directly they have passed the next corner.

The person who gives the commands may be one of the platoon leaders, or he may be someone who does not take part in the manoeuvres but acts solely as a Master of Ceremonies; in which case he should stand with his back to one of the short sides, leaving enough room for the riders to pass behind him.

Commands may refer to: (a) one platoon, (b) both platoons, (c) first section, (d) second section, (e) both first, or second, sections, (f) men individually, (g) women individually. In the first two cases the riders follow their platoon leader. In the next three instances they follow their section leader. In the last two cases they all work individually. The preparative order, 'Ladies, individual circle ...' or 'Circle singly ...' means that every woman makes her own circle when the executive order, 'Ride!' is given.

It is absolutely essential that if the command instructs the riders to follow their leader, then they must do so, even if the leader makes a series of ghastly mistakes. Anything is better than breaking the uniformity. 'Follow and ride on', should be the motto. All commands must be given clearly and slowly.

As in naval manoeuvres, it is most important to keep station, which means maintaining relative position and speed. The leader of the first platoon should set the pace. When riding 'spaced out' — not in close formation, but distributed at equal distances round the arena — the leader of the second platoon should keep station on him. If the sections in a platoon ride abreast, the platoon leader has the leader of the second section at his side, the other members of both sections forming up behind the leaders. The leaders leave about a yard between their horses. When riding abreast, the inside riders base their position on the outside riders, who can help them considerably by riding a little faster when turning in a circle, and by cutting the corners a little fine when riding round a square.

When platoons are riding at some distance from each other, the leader must take particular care to keep station. When they are riding round the track of a manège or school, there should always be a distance equal to the length plus the breadth of the arena between the leaders. If this rule is followed they are bound to reach the half-way mark or the diagonals at exactly the same time. Fig. 39 shows this quite clearly.

Directly the correct distance begins to get lost, steps must be taken to put the position right. Leaders should help each other by cutting corners or slowing down.

In Fig. 40 you can see two platoons riding spaced out, each divided into two sections. The sections are riding abreast. The leaders are A1, B1, C1, D1. Here A1 and C1 watch each other and their relative position, planning to arrive at the centre line at exactly the same time. A2 and A3 keep station on A1, B2 and B3 on B1, and so on. As the leaders are on the outside they should ride a little faster at the turns, otherwise the inside riders may have to drop back from a canter to a trot, or from a trot to a walk, which looks very bad.

Let us suppose that the next command is 'By threes, right . . . turn!' The inside riders, numbers 3 and 2 in each section on the plan, slow down while number 1 increases his pace. If the order was 'By threes, left about . . . turn!' they would be following the track in the opposite direction and number 3 would be on the outside in each section; station would then be kept on him. The change in the rider on whom station is kept always comes into effect on the centre line, so in this case station would be kept on number 1 until the centre line was next reached.

Various other figures bring about a change in leaders; for instance, the movement shown in Fig. 41. Here a platoon of six riders is following the track on the off rein. At the command 'Right . . . turn!' each rider immediately turns to the right, so that, instead of travelling in line ahead down one side of the arena, they find themselves travelling in line abreast across the arena. A further 'Right . . . turn!' at the other side brings them into line ahead once more travelling back down the length of the arena, still on the off rein but with number 6 in the lead.

Although leaders of a platoon, and even of a section, may change in this way, the platoon itself, and the sections in the platoon, remain the same, with the same riders and the same numbers. When two platoons or sections meet on the centre line and are required to continue through the ranks of an oncoming platoon or section, then each rider turns aside to his right allowing his opposite number to pass to his left.

This 'passing through' movement can be accomplished on the

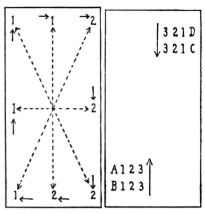

39 (left) Spacing of platoon leaders.
40 (right) Positioning of platoons.

The term 'dressing' is used for the procedure where the leaders glance inwards to check each other's position.

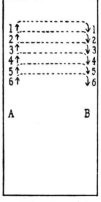

41 Changing platoon leaders by turning in line abreast.

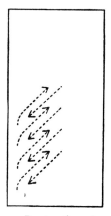

42 Passing through on the diagonal.

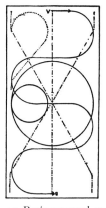

43 Basic carrousel movements.

The standard definition of a volte (or volt) in metric measurement is 6–8 m.

diagonal, as in Fig. 42. Let us suppose that the two platoons are riding spaced out, that is on opposite sides of the arena, on the off rein. The order 'Change rein along the diagonal!' is given. As the platoons approach each other down the diagonal, the order 'Open .. ranks!' is given, and the riders of each platoon make room for the other to pass through their ranks.

There are various schools of thought on which way to turn. Some are of the opinion that one should turn aside according to the rein on which one is riding; if one is riding on the right rein, then one turns to the right. Current opinion, however, considers it best to turn aside in the direction in which one *will* travel. So, in the example quoted above, since the riders *were* on the off rein when ordered to change, they *will come* on to the near rein and therefore move aside to the left. This is sensible, for it should eliminate the possibility of the leaders of a long column becoming blocked by the wall. Even if a delayed order is given to change rein, one would still move in the direction which is contained in the order. In other words, if, while crossing the arena, one is ordered to change rein on arriving at the other side, one would still move aside in the direction suggested in the order, on meeting another rider, although the order would not be put into effect until he had been passed.

CARROUSEL MOVEMENTS

Carrousel riding is based entirely on movements or figures, and riders are constantly trying to work out fresh variations by combining various moves. Here are the basic figures, which can be seen drawn in Fig. 43.

VOLTE. This means a circle about 20 ft in diameter, or rather less than half the width of the school.

CHANGE REIN. This, of course, means changing direction, but it is achieved in the following way: the rider passes a corner, and when it lies a horse's length behind him he turns down the diagonal; then, a horse's length from the far corner, he turns the opposite way, which takes him back to the track but travelling in the opposite direction.

LEFT ABOUT TURN. If this order is given on the near rein, i.e. when the rider has the wall of the school, or rails of the arena, on his right, he turns a half circle to the left, and then rides on a short diagonal course back to the track. If the order is given when on the off rein, i.e. the wall or rail is to the left, then the

Quadrille riders executing a volte. East Yorkshire Riding Club at the Horse of the Year Show. (Bob Langrish)

The Great Circle. Riders of Saumur. (Bob Langrish)

rider must first ride out from the wall on a short diagonal, then turn (see dotted line). Turning right about, the movements are the opposite.

GREAT CIRCLE. This is a circle with a diameter equal to the width of the school.

HALF SCHOOL CIRCLE. A circle half the size of the Large Circle.

A Great Circle (or Large Circle, as Lijsen also calls it) would normally be a 20 m circle if the work is performed in a standard dressage arena.

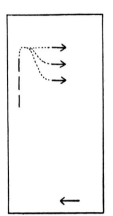

44 Coming into line.

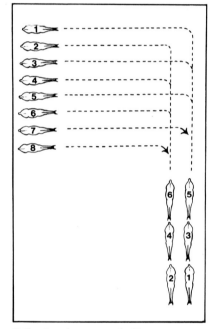

Following the command, 'From the left, break off by twos'.

CHANGE REIN ON THE 'S'. The rider describes half a Half School Circle, and on crossing the centre line changes rein to form a semi-circle in the opposite direction, thus tracing the shape of the letter 'S'.

COME INTO LINE. This order is given when the riders are in Indian file, they turn away from the wall forming up in line abreast at right angles to the way in which they were travelling. If on the off rein, as in Fig. 44, they form up on the leader's right; if on the near rein, then on the leader's left.

FROM THE LEFT, BREAK OFF BY TWOS, FOLLOW TRACK, OFF REIN. The riders are in line abreast, the pair on the left wing come forward, and, turning right, pass in front of the other and on down the track. As the rear legs of the first pair pass the second horse left in line abreast, the second pair break off and follow the first pair, and so on.

CROSS SINGLY. This has already been described. It means that while travelling in line ahead each rider makes a turn to left or right which brings them into line abreast. A further turn at the far side puts them into reverse order, line ahead, but travelling on the same rein as before, as in Fig. 45. It can also be made down the length of the school, when the order is given on a short side, as in Fig. 46. Fig. 47 shows two platoons passing through each other's ranks, for the order has been given when the platoons were on opposite sides of the arena. Each rider has pulled over to the right if he has been riding on the left rein, or to the left if he has been riding on the right.

TURN INSIDE, SINGLY, WITH CENTRE CIRCLE. This movement can best be seen in Fig. 48. Each rider turns his horse in towards the centre of the school and, on the centre line, turns

45 Cross singly: across the school.
46 Cross singly: down the length of the school.
47 Passing through across the arena.
48 Turn inside, singly, with centre circle.

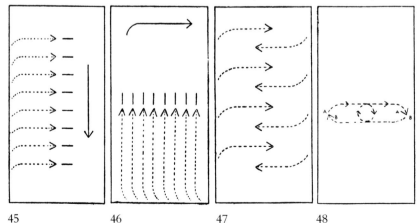

45   46   47   48

a small circle then continues to the opposite wall, remaining on the same rein.

TO THE CENTRE, LEFT (OR RIGHT) ABOUT TURN, AND BACK TO TRACK. One rides to the centre line and turns about — right upon the off rein, left on the near — then rides back to the track and turns to continue along it as before.

SHORT CHANGE. This starts in exactly the same way as changing along the diagonal, but only half the length is used, the movement ends on the centre line, as in Fig. 49.

BIG FIGURE-OF-EIGHT. This should take up the whole of the school. Starting half-way along a short side a semicircle is described which takes one to the centre, here one changes rein and rides a whole circle which fills half the school, on reaching the centre one changes rein again and completes the first circle, ending at the spot from which one started. It can be seen in Fig. 50.

REVERSE EIGHT. This can best be seen in Fig. 51, where the movements are shown for two sections of one platoon. It should, of course, be performed by two platoons simultaneously. These ride spaced out at an equal distance round the arena. The two platoons follow the figure shown in the diagram, each at the end of a diagonal.

Assuming that the platoon is riding on the near rein, the movements are as follows: On the order 'Reverse Eight ... Ride!' the first section rides a semicircle, the diameter of which equals half the width of the school, on the near rein. They then travel on a diagonal back to the wall, where they ride another semicircle, this time on the off rein. A second diagonal course brings them back to the wall. They have, in fact, made a simple figure-of-eight. The second section have to make a similar figure inside this, simultaneously, but in the opposite direction. So, at the command, they first leave the wall on a diagonal and when they come to the correct place (which can easily be seen, for the first section will either have just passed or still be passing), they wheel round in a semicircle on to the off rein; on regaining the wall they set off on the other diagonal, wheel round in a semicircle on the near rein, and so come back to their starting point. When passing each other the riders of the first section should turn to the outside.

SMALL EIGHT. As you can see in Fig. 52, this is a figure-of-eight made across the school.

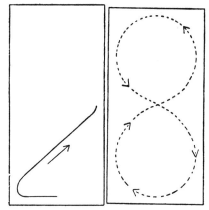

49 (left) Short change of rein.
50 (right) Big figure of eight.

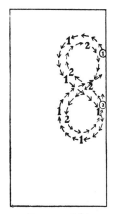

51 Reverse eight.

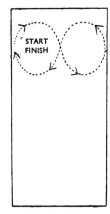

52 Small eight.

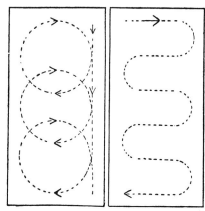

53 (left) Three circles.
54 (right) Serpentine.

THREE CIRCLES. These are turned successively on reaching the quarter mark, the half-way mark and the three-quarter mark, as shown in Fig. 53. On completion the riders follow the track.

SERPENTINE. The leader must first decide how many turns he is going to make. He then divides the length of the arena into twice this number and thus gets the radius of the semicircles he must turn. As can be seen in Fig. 54, the movement should be started at the centre of a short side; and the semicircles which are turned at alternate long sides are joined by straight lines. It is useful to remember that if there are an even number of turns, at the finish the platoon will automatically have changed rein.

BY THREES TO THE RIGHT AND CHANGE PLACES. This order can be given for any number and in either direction. It might easily be 'By twos ... to the left'. Fig. 55, however, shows 'by threes ... to the right ... change places!' The purpose of the movement is to get the outside rider on the inside and vice versa, when two or more riders are riding abreast. It is achieved by each horseman turning a semicircle to the right, on approaching the end of the school, so that he, who was on the outside, is now on the inside; and he, who was on the inside, now comes on the outside, as they travel on the same rein down the long wall opposite the point at which the order was given.

Three abreast with a platoon leader. Hillsborough Mounted Police, Tampa, Florida. (Bob Langrish)

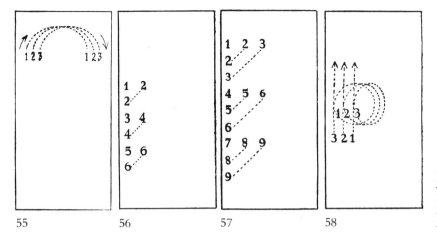

55

56

57

58

55 By threes to the right and change places.
56 Two abreast, or by twos.
57 Three abreast, or by threes.
58 Circle by threes and change places.

TWO ABREAST, OR BY TWOS ... (from Indian file). As Fig. 56 shows, the even numbers come up alongside the odd numbers immediately in front of them.

THREE ABREAST, OR BY THREES. The platoon should be numbered first, and each rider must remember his number. In each group of three, the second and third rider come up alongside the first. See Fig. 57.

LINE UP ON CENTRE LINE, BY PAIRS. The movement shown in Fig. 44 can be applied to pairs riding abreast. Each pair comes up to the same spot before wheeling round and moving down the centre line to turn into a single line abreast. Great care should be taken to see that the spacing is equal. The distance between pairs must be the same as the distance between the members of each pair.

CIRCLE BY THREES AND CHANGE PLACES. As can be seen in Fig. 58, the three riders are abreast; they circle to the right and, in so doing, reverse their order. Actually only number 2 makes a perfect circle, the course followed by numbers 1 and 3 is more like an ellipse.

FOUR CIRCLES. From the description this may seem rather complicated, but a glance at Fig. 59 should make it clear. The riders are in a column of pairs; that is to say, the second section of each platoon has ridden up alongside the first section. The platoons are evenly spaced round the school. When the order 'Centre short side, inside!' is given each platoon turns in down the centre line. But before they reach the half-way mark they are ordered 'By sections, right and left ... circle!' The horsemen on the left ride three-quarters of a circle to the left, then a whole

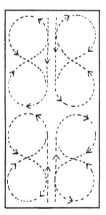

59 Four circles.

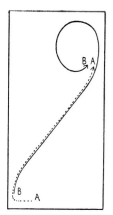

60 *First sections change and circle, second sections change rein.*

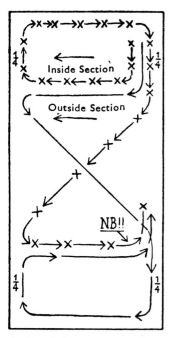

61 *Grand change.*

circle on the right rein and a quarter circle on the left, which should bring them back to their position, having made a figure-of-eight whose circles are half the width of the school in diameter. The riders on the right turn first to the right and afterwards ride a full circle on the near rein, before completing the figure-of-eight.

FIRST SECTIONS CHANGE AND CIRCLE. SECOND SECTIONS CHANGE REIN. These orders allow a section which has been following another to come up alongside a circle, the diameter of which is about half the width of the school, on the opposite rein. As the circle is completed they should fall in alongside the section which followed them down the diagonal. See Fig. 60.

GRAND CHANGE. You will find this easy to understand if you follow each move in Fig. 61. The riders are in a column of pairs. Let us suppose that they are on the off rein, and have just turned down a long side. At the quarter mark the order is given for the platoon to cross the school. The column therefore wheels right and travels across the school to the long wall opposite. Just before this is reached, the order is given to 'Break off for the Grand Change'. The pairs now split, forming two sections in Indian file. The section which was on the inside when moving up the long wall (shown by crosses in the diagram) wheels right and follows the track past two corners then *at the quarter mark* moves down the diagonal to change rein. This diagonal ends at the three-quarter mark, so that as they turn across the school they leave the remaining quarter clear for the manœuvres of the other section, with whom they should now join up. This outer section wheeled left at the order to break off, and immediately took the diagonal which led to the three-quarter mark on the opposite long wall, where they wheeled right and followed the track past two corners, and wheeled right again down the three-quarter line to join up with the other section, remaining on its outside, as both sections wheel left to follow the track, near rein.

LARGE CIRCLE IN THE CENTRE, ON BOTH REINS. The platoons are spaced out and in each the second section is riding alongside the first, giving us a column of pairs. Both platoons turn down the centre line towards each other. When they have travelled a quarter of the length of the school, the order 'Large circle, in the centre, on both reins' is given. Those riding on the right now wheel to the right and ride a circle on the near rein. Those on the left, wheel left and circle on the off rein. See Fig. 62. When passing, the first sections of each platoon go outside. Riders on the outside circle will have to ride a little faster since they have further to travel.

BREAK OFF AND RIDE TO THE FOUR CORNERS. This usually follows the movement described above. Directly the riders have passed each other, opposite the short sides of the school, each section turns towards the long wall in front of the leader and changes rein on the diagonal as can be seen in Fig. 63. This will lead each section round one corner and down a short side at the centre of which they will meet the other section of their platoon. Here they can join up and turn down the centre line once more.

FOUR CIRCLES WITH CHANGE. For this we must imagine that the large square which forms the centre of the school is subdivided into four smaller squares whose sides are equal to half the short side of the school. The riders are in single file; the sections are spaced out. Let us suppose that the riders are on the off rein. At the command each section will ride a semicircle to the right, the diameter of which is equal to half the width of the school. Then, passing into the next small square, they turn one and a quarter circles to the left. On completing this the riders pass into the third square and turn three-quarters of a circle to the right. They move into the fourth square to describe a circle and a quarter to the left and back into the first square to join up with the semicircle with which they started and made to the right. This can be seen in Fig. 64.

CHANGING REIN BY SECTIONS AND CHANGING AGAIN AT THE CENTRE. The riders move two by two, in sections evenly spaced out. At the order to change rein, the sections ride towards each other down the diagonal. When they are about four yards apart, the order 'Break off and change' is given. As the riders meet they turn off to left and right back down the other diagonal as shown in Fig. 65. Then each horseman follows the track with his new partner.

CHANGING REIN AND PASSING THROUGH. The horsemen ride either in pairs or fours and the sections are spaced out. At the order to change, the sections move towards each other down a diagonal. As they approach, the order 'Open ranks' is given and the sections pass through each other and then close ranks (Fig. 42).

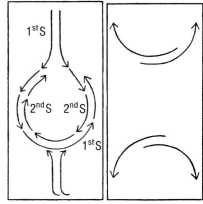

62 (left) Large circle in the centre, on both reins.
63 (right) Break off and ride to the four corners.

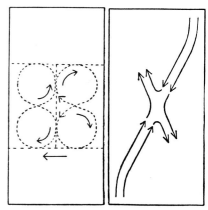

64 (left) Four circles with change.
65 (right) Changing rein by sections and changing again at the centre.

Windmill with 32 riders. Royal Canadian Mounted Police at Windsor. (Bob Langrish)

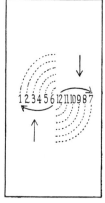

66 The Windmill.

67 The Windmill with 64 riders in a grand quadrille organised by the author in Holland.

FIGURES ON THE GREAT CIRCLE

THE WINDMILL. The riders travel round the Great Circle in single file. At the order to form the Windmill, the riders of each platoon form a radial line, with the platoon leaders keeping diametrically opposite each other (Fig. 66). They obviously ride very much faster than the inside horsemen who remain close together, facing opposite ways. If there were two platoons of six riders, then they would sweep round the circle like the sails of a windmill in this order: 1, 2, 3, 4, 5, 6, centre point, 12, 11, 10, 9, 8, 7; numbers 1 and 7 being the platoon leaders and the rest taking up their positions on them. If you divide your company into four sections or use four platoons, you can reproduce a windmill with four sails; see Fig. 67, a photograph which shows 64 riders taking part.

BREAK OFF SINGLY FROM CENTRE. RIDE SPACED OUT ON GREAT CIRCLE. The inside riders take the shortest route to the Great Circle and the rest follow, as in Fig. 68. Because, in forming the Windmill, the riders come up from behind, and now, in returning to the circle, continue in the same direction, they naturally pass the leaders, who remain on the circle all the time, and so the company is now in the reverse order. To bring them into the correct order you can either order them to turn about, which will put them on the other rein, or you can form another Windmill with 6 and 12 on the outside and 1 and 7 at the centre as in Fig. 69. When they break off to the circumference of the circle this time they will be in the correct order on the same rein.

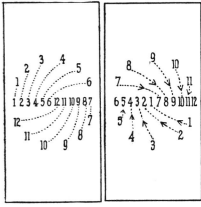

68 (left) *Break off singly from the centre.*
69 (right) *Reforming the Windmill.*

EVEN RIDERS CHANGE PLACES. The even riders pull in towards the centre and pass the rider in front as in Fig. 70. Timing is particularly important here as the riders should all leave their old position and arrive in the new at the same time. The quicker the speed, the more sharply will the rider have to turn. The order is sometimes given by the French word 'Remplacez'.

UNEVEN RIDERS CHANGE PLACES. This will bring them back into the right order.

PLATOONS CHANGE PLACES, FANWISE. This starts in exactly the same way as the Windmill, but instead of the riders forming up in line abreast on the diagonal each continues to ride across the circle to take up the position on the far side.

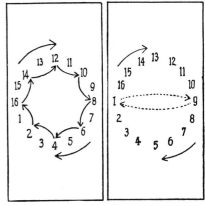

70 (left) *Even riders change places.*
71 (right) *Platoons change places singly.*

PLATOONS CHANGE PLACES SINGLY. Suppose that there are 16 riders evenly spaced round the Great Circle. At this order, 1 and 9 change places followed by 2 and 10, then 3 and 11, etc. (Fig. 71).

SERPENTINE. The riders are evenly spaced on the Great Circle, in Indian file, and, let us say, travelling on the right rein. Even numbers are now ordered to turn about so that they form an inner circle riding on the left rein (Fig. 72). On the command 'Serpentine . . . Ride!' (or, if you like, 'Grand Chain!' for that is what it is) the even numbers first turn outside and odd numbers turn inside. This starts the Grand Chain in which riders pass alternately on the outside and the inside as the two circles weave in and out. Finally the riders on the left rein are ordered to turn about and rejoin the Great Circle.

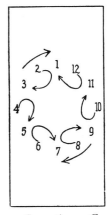

72 *Serpentine or Grand Chain.*

SPACING OUT PLATOONS AND SECTIONS

FIRST METHOD. While travelling along the long side, the first platoon wheels across the centre of the arena, and wheels again on the opposite side to continue on the same rein. The second platoon describes a circle which will bring it back to the point at which the first platoon turned off just as the first platoon wheels back on to the track at the far side. In this way they will be diametrically opposite each other. To space out the sections, the first section should continue its way while the second section turns a circle whose circumference is equal to half a long side plus half a short side of the arena.

SECOND METHOD. Both platoons ride side by side. Half-way down the long wall they wheel across the school. On arriving at the centre they wheel left and right; when they reach the short walls they wheel so that they are both on the same rein. This can be seen in Fig. 73.

THIRD METHOD. Both platoons ride side by side. Half-way along the short side the inner one wheels down the centre line, at the centre wheels again, and at the wall wheels a third time all in the same direction. Meanwhile the outside section continues along the track, as shown in Fig. 74.

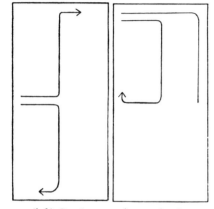

73 (left) Spacing out platoons by the second method.

74 (right) Spacing out platoons by the third method.

GARLAND MANŒUVRES

The Garland Manœuvre has great charm and will amply repay studying. Each garland is made of a cane 12−15 ft long, around which artificial flowers are twined. You can see the effect in Fig. 75. The first thing you must do is to make your horse accustomed to the garlands. It is no use rehearsing with undecorated canes; the

75 The garland manœuvre.

garlands must be complete from the start, otherwise you will only have to start all over again when you put the flowers on. The most important point for riders to remember is to hold the canes in a vertical position. Here is a simple but most effective routine.

Each garland is held by two riders. (It is possible for every rider to have a garland, but this requires more skill, as the rider has to hold both ends of the garland as well as his reins.) The ends of the garlands are held in the outside hands of each pair of riders. The inside hands hold the reins which should be from a simple snaffle, without the curb.

1. The riders enter in pairs at the walk, along the long side of the arena, opposite the spectators' stand.

2. Half-way along they turn left, if they are on the left rein, across the arena towards the grandstand in line abreast. On the centre line they halt and salute the spectators. This should be done by numbers: on 'One' the garlands are raised at arm's length and on 'Two' they are lowered. This will ensure that all the performers work in perfect unison.

3. They move on, and immediately in front of the stands they turn left along the track, so that they continue round the arena on the left rein, but now the last pair lead. This can be seen in Fig. 41, but performed on the right rein.

4. Change rein on the diagonal.

5. Each pair turns right across the arena and right at the other side to follow the track.

6. Half-way along a short side they turn down the centre line.

7. On reaching the end, uneven pairs turn to the left, even pairs to the right. Change rein and pass through (Fig. 76).

8. Half-way along the short side, as the pairs come together again, they turn down the centre line, and at the end all wheel right and follow the track.

9. Open the ranks.

10. Change places (see Figs. 75 and 77). This is accomplished as follows: The last pair of riders lower the garland so that it lies horizontally behind them and ride as quickly as possible through the lines, under all the other garlands, up to the front, where they immediately raise their garland to form the last arch for the next pair to ride through. This continues until the leading pair is again in front.

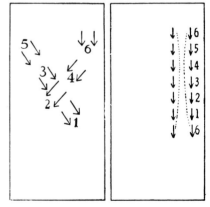

76 *(left) Changing rein in pairs and passing through.*
77 *(right) Changing places.*

78 Pairs of riders behind each other so that garlands run 'fore and aft'.

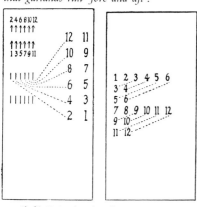

79 (left) Pairs break off and follow track, two deep and six abreast.
80 (right) Form sections, line abreast.

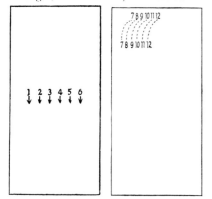

81 (left) Down the arena in line abreast.
82 (right) Turn right into line ahead.

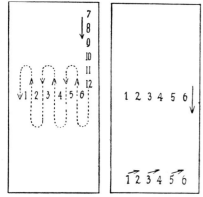

84 (left) Second sections serpentines between members of first section.
85 (right) Second section continues round the track, first section rides forward and takes the left track.

11. Close ranks.
12. Pairs break off and follow the track two deep, six abreast. If you study Figs. 78 and 79 you will see that all the men form the front rank and the women the rear. The garlands, therefore, now run 'fore and aft'.
13. Break off and regain position of pairs in line ahead.
14. Repeat movement 12.
15. Repeat movement 13.
16. Form sections line abreast, inward. The first pair remains on the track, the second pair comes up on their inside, the third pair on the inside of the second pair. The fourth, fifth and sixth pairs ride directly behind the first three pairs, as in Fig. 80.
17. The first section, 1, 2, 3, 4, 5, 6, turn down the length of the arena when they reach the centre line, still in line abreast and come to a halt as in Fig. 81. They must allow enough space between them for a horse to pass through.
18. Meanwhile the other section continues in line abreast until, on reaching a short side, it receives the order to turn right into line ahead, as in Fig. 82.
19. The second section 'serpentines' in and out between members of the first section. Figs. 83 and 84 show this quite plainly.
20. While the second section rides round the track in line ahead, the first section is ordered to ride forward and follow the track on the left rein, as in Fig. 85.
21. Second section comes up in pairs as in Fig. 86.
22. The first section turns in pairs to the left and closes up; the second section crosses and closes up so as to follow on behind the first.

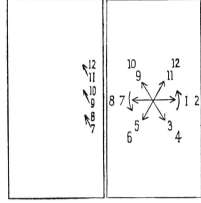

23. Great Circle, in the centre, evenly spaced. The first pair, looking across the centre of the circle should see the fourth pair directly opposite them, as in Fig. 87.
24. Change places by sections, in pairs. The first and fourth pairs change, then the second and fifth, finally the third and sixth.
25. The Windmill (Fig. 88).

86 (left) Turning in pairs to the left.
87 (right) Great Circle in pairs.

88 The Windmill.

26. From the centre, move in pairs to the Great Circle. This is shown in Fig. 89.
27. Repeat movement 25.
28. Repeat movement 26. These repeats are necessary to get the riders back into the correct order.
29. The Cupola (Fig. 90). The first pair ride to the centre, where number 1 stops but number 2 rides on and swings round to face him, still holding the garland, which now forms an arch over the necks of both horses. This can be seen in Fig. 91. Number 3 now comes up on number 1's left, while number

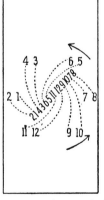

89 From the Windmill in pairs to the Great Circle.

90 The Cupola.

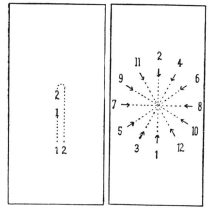

91 (left) Pairs face each other to form an arch.
92 (right) Forming a circle for the Cupola.

4 rides on to come up on number 2's left. The other pairs follow so that they form a circle, the garlands arching over and crossing, *at the highest point*, to form the Cupola, as in Fig. 92.

30. Salute, by numbers as in movement 2.
31. Break from the Cupola in pairs and follow the track on the left rein.
32. Turn left to cross the arena facing the spectators in line abreast.
33. Halt.
34. Salute as before.
35. From the right wing, in pairs, move forward to the track, turn right and exit on the right rein.

THE RIBBON MANŒUVRE

The Ribbon Manœuvre is really only suitable for an indoor riding school or the circus ring. From the roof, ribbons of different colours hang down, each is held in the hand of a rider. As the manœuvre progresses the ribbons seem to get in such a complicated knot that it would appear impossible to get them unravelled. But, like the Maypole dances, it is really much simpler than it looks.

Although, on the Continent, there are various forms of elaborate apparatus for this manœuvre, two bicycle wheels are all that are really required, apart from the ribbons. If possible one of the wheels should be smaller than the other. The wheels, the smaller underneath, revolve separately but both are parallel to the ground; the spindle is therefore vertical. The ribbons are 4 in. wide and long enough to reach from the wheel to a rider on the Large Circle and leave 6 ft to spare. One end is tied to the wheel, the other is finished with a loop. The rider's left hand holds the loop and the reins. The right hand raises the ribbon as necessary. If there are eight riders, then four ribbons of one colour are fastened to one wheel and four of a contrasting colour are fastened to the other wheel.

Here is a manœuvre for eight or more riders.

The riders enter in pairs, at the walk, on the right rein, and space themselves equally round the Great Circle.

1. In pairs, turn right, and move to the centre. Halt.
2. Take up the ribbons. These should be handed by an attendant, who distributes the colours alternately.
3. The riders move back to the Great Circle and trot round evenly spaced.
4. Form sections. Number 1 (white) has 2 (blue), 3 (white) and 4 (blue) on his right. Behind them come the second section: 5 (white) behind 1, with 6 (blue), 7 (white) and 8 (blue) to his right behind 2, 3 and 4.
5. First section change places, so that number 4 rides outside and number 1 rides inside. Numbers 2 and 3 also change.
6. The second section change places so that white comes to the outside.
7. Circle by sections, and change places. Blue outside.
8. Circle by sections, and change places. Forward single file, white in front.
9. Horsemen with blue ribbons ride in a circle, followed by those with white ribbons.
10. Those with white ribbons ride in a circle, and are followed by those with blue.
11. Individual right-about turns.
12. Blue ribbons are followed by white, riding in a circle.
13. White ride in a circle, and are followed by blue.
14. Form sections as in movement 4. Blue to come on the outside.
15. Circle by sections, and change places.
16. Second section change places, so that blue comes outside.
17. First section change places.
18. Circle by sections, sections change places and ride in Indian file on the Great Circle.

19. Individual left-about turns. Walk, then canter.
20. Form sections, blue to the outside.
21. Move across the ring by sections, change places and break off in pairs, blues to blues, whites to whites.
22. Forward in single file, two blues followed by two whites, etc.
23. Number 2's change places so that they come in front of number 1's.
24. Number 1's change places so that they come in front of number 2's.
25. Form sections; white to the outside.
26. The first sections change places and break off, blue coming before white.
27. Second section follows suit.
28. Blues change places.
29. Whites change places. All walk.
30. Individual right-about turns.
31. Whites change places.
32. Blues change places.
33. Second section change places and form a new section with white on the outside.
34. First section moves into Indian file, blue leading.
35. Number 1's change places.
36. Number 2's change places.
37. Circle in pairs by colours, blues together, whites together.
38. Form sections.
39. Ride in Indian file.
40. Individually turn left to the centre.
41. Halt.
42. Hand in the ribbons.

QUADRILLES

Quadrilles were often based on actual dances for four couples.

An act of great distinction is *La Quadrille des Lanciers*, with riders dressed in Louis XIV costume, wearing powdered wigs and tricornes. But here I would like to give readers a word of warning. Do not think that you can make your own wigs out of cotton wool or white crêpe hair. It is far better to hire wigs, and men will look better if they hire naturally coloured wigs already powdered, not dead white.

The ladies should, if possible, ride side-saddle; in which case their position is on their partners' left; if they ride astride, then they ride on their partners' right.

Eighteenth-century costume very suitable for a quadrille. John Lassetter's Lipizzaners at Goodwood. (Bob Langrish)

It is advisable to rehearse the moves thoroughly on foot first. If the mounted quadrille is ridden in exactly the same way as the dance, you may well find that the performance takes too long. It is best, therefore, to cut out some of the repetitive movements and figures. If, for instance, the movement known as *Les Tiroirs* is performed by the first two gentlemen with the third and fourth ladies, these can remain standing while the others perform a *different* movement.

Here then is a special quadrille, based on the correct movements of the dance. If the ladies are riding side-saddle, right should be read as left, and vice versa.

The first pair stand facing the orchestra, opposite the third pair, who have their backs to the music. The second pair are to the right of the first pair, and the fourth are to the left. The numbers, therefore, run anticlockwise.

SALUTE. Each gentleman raises his hat, with outstretched arm, to his partner. The ladies acknowledge this with a nod, *not a bow!*

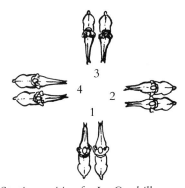

Starting position for La Quadrille des Lanciers. The 'orchestra' or grandstand is behind the third pair.

The pairs now ride towards the centre where the gentlemen all turn left and ride in a circle on the off rein, while the ladies turn right and circle on the near rein; as the gentlemen pass each lady they raise their hats in salute. The gentleman of the first pair will first meet the lady of the fourth pair, then the lady of the third pair, next the lady of the second pair and finally his own partner.

LE DORSET OR LES TIROIRS.   The gentleman of the first and the lady of the third pair now ride towards each other. The gentleman salutes as he passes the lady to the left at the centre. Both then turn left about, and regain their original places, passing behind their partners, thus approaching their own positions from the rear. Other riders follow suit.

LA RONDE.   In this the riders simply canter round the Great Circle on the right rein, evenly spaced, and return to their normal positions.

LES LIGNES OR DODOISKA.   The first pair ride forward, turn right and circle round the second pair. They then move across and circle round the back of the fourth pair to come up on their left. Here the gentleman of the first pair leaves his partner on the left of the gentleman of the fourth pair, while he rides to the centre of the ring, turns, salutes the three he has just left, turns left again and rides towards the second pair, salutes, passes behind them and comes up on their right, that is next the lady, and facing his own partner across the ring. The two ladies and one gentleman circle round to the right, while the two gentlemen and one lady circle round to the left. Both trios then move forward to the centre and, while they salute, the gentlemen escort their own partners back to their original positions by riding in a circle to the left. The other pairs can then follow suit.

LES MOULINETS OR LA NATIVE.   The lady of the first pair rides to the centre and stops. The gentleman of the third pair

An attractive movement in a quadrille. Wilmslow and District Riding Club performing right and left shoulder-in on the centre line at the Horse of the Year Show. (Bob Langrish)

rides towards her, stops, salutes, and returns to his original position by riding in a circle to the right. As he starts to go back to his place the other three ladies ride forward to the centre and all four ride in a close circle, one behind the other, to the right. The gentlemen circle to the left on the outside. Each one salutes his partner when meeting her. At a given signal, he rides back with her to their original position. The lady of the second pair then rides forward and is met by the gentleman of the fourth pair to start the routine again. The ladies of third and fourth pairs can follow suit.

LA RONDE. As previously described.

LES VISITES. The first pair rides forward in a small circle and stops in front of the second pair, salutes, passes left around this pair and straight across to the fourth pair, stopping near the centre of the circle. They salute, and both pairs one and four then ride the Windmill figure in the centre. The fourth pair stop in their correct position, the first pair ride on round and come up in front of the fourth pair, salute, and return to their place. Other pairs can follow suit.

GRAND CHAIN. As in dancing the Lancers there is a Grand Chain. The gentlemen turn left and ride round in a circle to the outside on the right rein, the ladies turn right and circle inside on the left rein. Both are evenly spaced. After one circuit has been completed, the riders on meeting pass each other first to the left, then to the right, then left, and so on. All riders should watch the horseman in front so that the turns are made at the same moment, as in Fig. 93.

LA RONDE. As before.

PROMENADE. The first pair ride forward, and turn right about some three or four lengths in front of the third pair so that they face the same way. The second pair ride forward and take up their position immediately behind the first pair; the fourth pair ride forward and take up their position between pairs 2 and 3. All ride forward; the ladies wheeling in a semicircle to the right and the gentlemen wheeling in a semicircle to the left. On meeting again, the gentlemen salute and ride forward at the side of their partners down the centre line. On reaching the centre of the ring the first pair ride straight ahead, while the second pair turn to the left and the third to the right. The hindmost pair stand still. In this way all four pairs are back in their original positions.

La Quadrille des Lanciers (see p. 116).

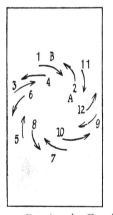

93 Forming the Grand Chain.

Circling into line abreast. East Yorkshire Riding Club, Horse of the Year Show. (Bob Langrish)

SALUTE. As in the first movement; the pairs then close up and come into line abreast in front of the grandstand.

THE GRAND QUADRILLE

This quadrille was arranged by the author, and ridden under his command by 64 riders at Le Concours Hippique at Hoofdoorp, and in the Amsterdam Stadium (Fig. 67).

Line up in front of the spectators.

1. Left turn and walk forward in pairs, wheeling on to the Great Circle.
2. Trot.
3. Inside platoon rides a big figure-of-eight.
4. Uneven pairs change places.
5. Even pairs change places.
6. Uneven sections (groups of 16) ride a circle with a diameter equal to half the width of the Great Circle.
7. Ride by fours.
8. Come up into eights.
9. Uneven eights circle on half the width.
10. Even eights circle on half the width.
11. The Windmill is then formed with four sails each made up of a group of 16.
12. Break off in pairs, and ride on the Great Circle.

13. Close up by fours.
14. Turn by fours.
15. Uneven fours to the left, even fours to the right.
16. Change rein along the diagonal and pass through.
17. Turn in down the centre, by eights.
18. Uneven eights to the left, even eights to the right.
19. Turn in down the centre by sixteens.
20. Uneven sixteens to the left, even sixteens to the right.
21. Turn in down the centre by thirty-twos.
22. Uneven thirty-two to the left, even thirty-two to the right.
23. By sixty-four, swing round into line abreast opposite the grandstand.
24. Halt.
25. Salute.

OBSTACLE QUADRILLE FOR EIGHT RIDERS

When you start rehearsing this quadrille you should lay four poles on the ground in the form of a cross, over which the horses have to step. When both horses and riders know their moves perfectly, low brush fences are substituted for the poles.

Before entering the arena, the riders are numbered so that each one knows whether he is 'odd' or 'even'. They enter at the canter, ride once round the school and come on to the Great Circle on the right rein, equally spaced.

1. Even riders change places.
2. Uneven riders change places.
3. Repeat 1.
4. Repeat 2.
5. Circle in pairs.
6. Even pairs change places.
7. Uneven pairs change places.
8. Repeat 6.
9. Repeat 7.
10. Even pairs circle.
11. Uneven pairs circle.
12. By pairs, right turn, passing left.
13. By pairs, right turn.
14. Even pairs through the centre. They jump simultaneously in opposite directions, one pair over the left obstacle, the other over the right. They should jump simultaneously.

15. The Star. This is formed by the horsemen riding their mounts into the four angles formed by the jumps. All the horses' heads face in towards the centre.
16. Salute.

BOLERO QUADRILLE

This quadrille was ridden by eight students of Delft University in 1933 under the direction of the author. The company entered at the trot on the right rein, in pairs, consisting of a lady and a gentleman. As the performance took place in a circus ring, the riders found themselves immediately on the Great Circle, around which they spaced themselves at equal distances and came to a halt.

1. Ladies circle singly and regain their position.
2. Gentlemen circle singly and regain their position.
3. Change places, first 1 and 5, then 2 and 6, etc.
4. Gentlemen turn about so that they ride on an inner circle in the opposite direction to the ladies, who ride round on the outer circle.
5. Waltz. Here number 1 leads. When he meets his partner, all riders ride simultaneously in a very small circle, which amounts to a pirouette, head to tail. They then ride on until they meet the next rider when once more they turn. In all each couple should make four turns, as rapidly as possible.
6. All riders turn individually so that now the ladies come on the inner circle, and gentlemen on the outer.
7. Waltz. Repeat the previous movement, as in 5.
8. All ride on the Great Circle. Each lady makes a turn to fall in behind her partner.
9. Gentlemen ride diametrically across the ring, singly; as each one reaches the centre he turns in a small circle and then continues on his way.
10. Ladies perform a similar evolution.
11. Gentlemen change places. Each one rides ahead of the lady in front.
12. Ladies change places.
13. Come up into pairs.
14. Gentlemen ride a half-circle, form a square in the centre, head to tail, and stand still.
15. Ladies form a square in the centre. As the ladies move in, the

gentlemen ride back to the Great Circle.

16. Ladies make a half-turn and take up their correct positions on the Great Circle.
17. Come up in pairs.
18. Uneven pairs to the centre to form the Windmill.
19. Uneven pairs back to the Great Circle; even pairs to form the Windmill.
20. Uneven pairs to the Great Circle and change places.
21. Even pairs change places.
22. Come up into fours, then to the centre to form the Windmill.
23. Back to the Great Circle.
24. Repeat 22.
25. Repeat 23.
26. Come up into eight and halt.

TANDEM MANŒUVRES

As a matter of fact 'Tandem manœuvres' is not really an accurate name for what we are going to describe. Tandem should refer only to a pair when the leader is harnessed between traces. What we are going to describe is actually riding *à la flèche*. But now that bicycles are called tandems, perhaps one may be excused.

A tandem, with the leader being driven and the second horse mounted. Note that in this case the leader's reins are held on either side of the ridden horse's head. Circus Gruss. (David Jamieson)

Cisko, a variation of à la flèche riding, with three leaders and the rider standing on two horses. Also known as Chico's Post. The Hungarian Herdsmen at the Royal International Horse Show. (Bob Langrish)

When riding *à la flèche*, the leader is directed by the rider mounted on the horse which follows. Variations on this theme are brought about by the number and position of the horses in front of the rider. Sometimes one sees two or three horses (which are usually coupled together); these formations are known as *La Flèche roumaine* and the *Troika*. Usually the applause grows with the number of leaders, but really the enthusiasm of the spectators should decrease, for the greater the number of leaders, the easier they are to drive. No team of horses swings so easily off the course as does a single leader.

There is often much discussion on how the reins should be held. There are some who believe that the head of the horse they are riding should be held between the reins which control the leader; but this is wrong. Let us suppose that the horses are to wheel round. The saddle horse must not start to turn until he has reached the place where the leader wheeled, but that cannot be achieved if the saddle horse's head is between the reins of the leader.

The proper way to hold the reins is as follows. On the right rein the leader's reins come to the right of the saddle horse, on the left rein they come to the left. This means that when you change rein you must also bring the leader's reins round to the other side of the saddle horse's head.

The saddle horse should be ridden on the snaffle only. If a curb is used the leader's reins may get between the bars of the curb, which can be very dangerous. The reins of the saddle horse are usually divided by either the third or little finger of the left hand. Before setting out the rider should measure his reins and not alter them during the ride (Fig. 94).

At the end of the leader's reins, which should be of precisely the right length, there should be a small loop, through which the little finger of the left hand can be inserted. This will prevent the reins from hanging down too far. It has happened that a rider's boot has become entangled in the reins, and it is possible for the saddle horse to step over them if they hang too low.

The leader's left rein should lie between the thumb and index finger of the left hand; the right should lie between the third and little finger of the right hand. The whip is held in the palm of the right hand, rising from the thumb and with about four inches of handle showing below the little finger.

The Golden Rule of riding *à la flèche* is that the saddle horse shall follow precisely the footsteps of the leader.

If the saddle horse and leader turn at the same time, then the saddle horse — and the whip — come up inside the leader, which tends to make him move aside. This is not only ugly, but exactly the opposite of what is required.

Before applying the aid of the reins to the leader, both the rider's hands should be on the same side of the horse's neck as the direction in which he is travelling. If the horse is on the right rein, then both hands are on the right-hand side of the saddle horse's neck. The left hand presses slightly on the right side of the neck and keeps the horse straight, while the little finger of the right hand is brought slightly back. When the horse has to turn, the left hand is moved to the right, which makes the horse follow.

One of the most common mistakes, and one which accounts for so many 'loose' riders, is that the saddle horse comes up on the inside too soon. In turning the rider should always bring his horse *outside* the leader and remain behind. He should never try to bring the leader in front of the saddle horse; he must *follow*.

A mistake which can be made at the outset is to try and urge the leader forward before the saddle horse. This is quite wrong, for the leader will be pulled up short by the reins and become uneasy and nervous. First, the saddle horse should move, and

'The bars of the curb', or more usually the 'arms', i.e. the cheeks of the bit.

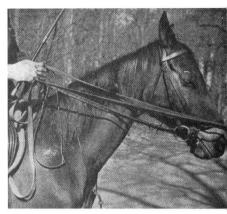

94 How to hold the reins of the leader and the saddle horse when riding tandem.

then the leader. The whip should be used most sparingly and applied only to the shoulder.

If the rider wants to canter he must first urge his own horse on, then the leader will move. When stopping, pull up the leader first, then your own.

Let us suppose that we want to change rein. We are on the right rein — so our hands are to the right of the horse's neck — and we want to change to the left. By bringing the horses a little more on the bit we make them attentive. In order to turn off the track the bridle hand is brought to the left, and the leader's left rein is slackened while the right hand presses on the right rein. The leader turns inside, but the saddle horse remains on the track. When we reach the point at which the leader turned off, the left hand is brought over to the right, and the saddle horse follows the leader. When we pass the centre of the school, we are on the other rein, both hands are therefore then moved to the other side of the neck. To accomplish this we take the leader's left rein between the thumb and index finger of the right hand (as in Fig. 95) and lift it over the saddle horse's head careful not to touch him in the process. When it lies on the left side it is taken in the left hand (Fig. 96).

The leader is thus warned of what is to come; we bring our horse a little over to the right, move the left hand to the left, and press on the left stirrup. It is at this point that one so often sees a loose leader, due entirely to the rider's coming up on the inside. If he then tries to put things right with the whip, he will only get into further trouble. So let us repeat the Golden Rules.

1. Never come up on the leader's inside; always turn round on his outside.
2. Never try to bring the leader in front of the saddle horse. (If you succeed it will be a miracle!) Let your leader go, remain quiet and ride quickly forward behind your leader's tail.
3. If the leader stops, give him rein and urge the saddle horse forward. (If the rider stops, then the leader and saddle horse start a tug-of-war, and the rider cannot win.)

In jumping *à la flèche*, remember that the leader must have a long rein when taking off. Before reaching the jump, the right hand takes the left rein and raises it over the saddle horse's head, no matter on which rein you are riding. When holding the right rein high you should bring it back, so that the distance between

Bridle hand, i.e. left hand.

95 Preparing to change from the right rein to the left rein.

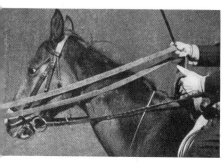

96 Completing the change from the right rein to the left rein.

This is a difficult movement.

An introduction to jumping in tandem. The brothers Alexis and Patrick Gruss. (David Jamieson)

the two horses becomes smaller. You will then be able to give the leader the extra rein he needs for jumping by bringing the right hand forward. After the obstacle has been cleared, the reins are again held in both hands.

The leader's reins can be shortened or lengthened while being held in the air.

A *flèche* rider always salutes by raising his whip so that it touches his cap and lies along the right-hand side of his nose.

MANŒUVRES FOR FLECHE RIDERS

A SIMPLE MANŒUVRE. For any multiple of four riders. They enter in single file on the right rein. At the middle of the long side they turn right, stop on the centre line and salute.

Each rider is mounted on one horse and drives one or more horses in front of him — usually three.

1. From the left wing they ride off on the right rein in single file.
2. Half-way along the short side they turn down the centre line.
3. At the far end of the centre line, uneven numbers to the left, even to the right.
4. Back at the short side, both turn down the centre line in single file.

5. By sections right wheel.
6. By sections right wheel.
7. By sections circle.
8. By sections circle.
9. First platoon turns to the right. Second platoon circle evenly spaced.
10. By platoons right turn.
11. Single, right turn and right again.
12. Great Circle.
13. By twos.
14. By fours.
15. Follow the track.
16. By fours right turn, break off and ride forward in single file.
17. Singly to the right.
18. Half-way along the short side, turn down the centre line.
19. At the far end, uneven riders to the left, even to the right; both change rein down the diagonal, passing through at the centre.
20. Half-way along the far short side, turn down the centre line once more.
21. Follow the track to the right.
22. Turn right into line abreast and stop along the centre line.
23. Salute.

MANŒUVRE FOR FOUR RIDERS. Enter at the walk on the right rein. Trot on.

1. The two riders of each section circle, keeping diametrically opposite each other.
2. By sections right turn.
3. By sections right wheel and circle in the centre of the school.
4. Come up into two deep along the track.
5. Change rein along the diagonal.
6. Repeat movement 5.
7. Uneven riders to the right, even riders circle, as in Fig. 97.
8. Repeat 7.
9. By sections right turn and close up.
10. Turn right in pairs and forward in fours.
11. Turn right in fours and forward in pairs.
12. Repeat 10.
13. Repeat 11, and go forward in single file.
14. Great Circle, evenly spaced.

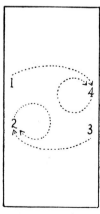

97 Uneven riders to the right, even riders circle.

15. 1 and 3 change places.
16. 2 and 4 change places.
17. Repeat 15.
18. Close up and follow the track.
19. Turn right and come up four abreast, as in Fig. 98.
20. Great Circle, in the centre, four abreast.
21. Circle.
22. Change places as in Fig. 99.
23. Repeat 22.
24. Follow the track, four abreast.
25. Turn down the centre line in single file; turn into line abreast; halt.
26. Salute.
27. From the left wing break off and follow at the walk to the exit.

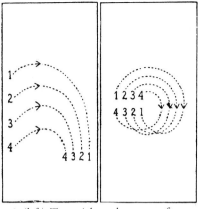

98 (left) Turn right and come up four abreast.
99 (right) Change places on the circle.

MANŒUVRE FOR FOUR RIDERS. In a circus ring the riders enter at the trot or canter.

1. 1 and 3 change places.
2. 2 and 4 change places.
3. 1 and 2 change places.
4. Ride in odd pairs, 1 with 4, and 2 with 3.
5. 3 and 2 change places.
6. 1 and 4 change places.
7. Repeat 5.
8. Repeat 6.
9. Come up in fours, line abreast 1, 4, 3, 2.
10. Circle and change places, 2, 3, 4, 1.
11. Repeat 10, bringing the order to 1, 4, 3, 2.
12. Repeat 10, bringing the order to 2, 3, 4, 1.
13. Repeat 10, bringing the order to 1, 4, 3, 2.
14. Stop.
15. Salute.
16. From the centre, move out in single file to the Great Circle, spaced out, on the right rein.
17. Leaders inside. The leaders come to the centre and trot in a small circle.
18. Leaders go back to the Great Circle.
19. Saddle horses inside. (The reins of the leaders are brought over to the other side.)
20. Saddle horses back to the Great Circle.

21. Waltz. The right hand takes the leader's right rein twelve inches nearer the bit, and so makes the leader turn. The saddle horse is urged forward, and the two horses turn, head to tail. Every time the leader comes back on the track he is urged forward, and another turn follows.
22. Stop waltz and follow the track.
23. Exit.

LOW SCHOOL ROUTINE

The Low School is ridden by any number of riders which is a multiple of four. They enter at the walk, come into line, salute in unison, and then ride the following routine; particular attention being paid to making the paces and figures correctly and with style.

The school is divided into four rectangles, each measuring half the width by half the length. The centre (or each corner of the rectangle, if you wish) can be marked with a tub of flowers.

The riders break off in such a way that, riding at the trot on the right rein, they each reach the half-way mark of the four walls at the same time. The routine proceeds as follows:

1. Once round the whole school, equally spaced.
2. Each circles in his own corner.
3. Each rides round his own small rectangle.
4. Ride down the short and long centre lines, so that the riders meet in the middle of the school, where they circle equally spaced.
5. Each rider turns right-about.
6. Follow the track round the school.
7. Figure-of-eight. Circle in the corners.
8. Follow the small rectangles.
9. Repeat movement 4.
10. Follow the big square.
11. Figure-of-eight.
12. *Travers*, along one long side.
13. Turn around the haunches.
14. Back in *renvers*.
15. As 12.
16. Half-pass.
17. *Renvers*, along one long side.
18. Walk on the long rein, and follow the track of the school.

This is a standard way of teaching young riders in a group lesson to ride in a confident and consistent manner. Some movements (such as half-pass) obviously need special lessons beforehand. See glossary for explanation of terms.

19. Bring your horses on the bit again.
20. Canter around the school.
21. Circle in the centre, closed up. The horses describe a small circle, almost head to tail.
22. Open circle, the circle is gradually widened.
23. Uneven riders form a figure-of-eight. At the centre they should change the canter in the air, if possible; otherwise they must bring the other leg into the lead by trotting an even number of paces.
24. Even riders form a figure-of-eight.
25. Close up.
26. Come up into fours.
27. Stop and salute.

GYMKHANA GAMES AND RACES

The Bending Race, Egg and Spoon Race, Potato Race and Relay Race are all well known; perhaps too well known, for although we may be fond of old favourites, we do like something new to bring a bit of originality to a gymkhana programme now and then. So here are twelve games and races from the Continent.

BATTLE OF THE HATS. The riders face each other in two rows of equal numbers. They wear top hats made of paper or papier mâché and are each armed with a paper-bound stick. When the whistle is blown, the two rows ride towards each other and try to knock their opponent's hat off. Competitors are not allowed to touch their hats with their hands. Whoever loses his hat has to retire, and the winner of that bout attacks someone else. The rider who keeps his hat on longest wins the prize.

SADDLE RACE. The competitors stand in a row, each holding a bareback horse. The saddles lie in a heap on the other side of the arena or school. When the whistle is blown, the competitors have to lead their horse to the saddles, saddle the horse and gallop back to the starting line. The first to arrive is the winner.

HORSE THIEVES' RACE. The horses stand in a group in the middle of the arena. They are saddled and the snaffle reins are passed under the stirrup leathers. The riders line up for the start and have to run to the horses, mount one and gallop round a set course. It is both more difficult and more amusing if the competitors are given umbrellas, which they have to open before they start running.

TALLY-HO RACE. A set course is marked out in sections and competitors are told at what pace each section must be covered: first trot, then canter, then walk, then gallop, etc. If any rider breaks into a pace which is faster than that allowed for that section of the course, he is penalized by being made to ride in a circle, or to dismount and mount again.

TILTING. A number of curtain rings are suspended on thin threads hanging down from a beam which spans the course. Riders take it in turns to either trot or canter under the beam and impale a ring on their 'lance', which is a length of bamboo or a hazel stick.

NEEDLE AND THREAD RACE. The men, already mounted, stand at one end of the course, each with a needle in his hand; the ladies stand at the other end each with a length of thread. When the tapes go up, the men gallop up to the ladies, dismount, give them the needle to thread and bring it back to the start, which is the winning post. A variation of this is to make the men thread the needle and the ladies to ride in the race.

Tilting at the ring. The tilting festival in Sønderborg, Denmark. (John Sommer/Danish Tourist Board)

SCHOLARS' RACE. This is a variation of the Needle and Thread Race. Instead of the needle the rider takes an envelope which contains a sum which the partner at the far end of the course has to do.

THE PYJAMA GAME. Competitors have to ride to the far end of the course, dismount, dress up in a suit of pyjamas and ride back.

TUMBLER RACE. This is a version of the Egg and Spoon Race. Tumblers of water replace the egg in the spoon, and the amount of water left in the glass denotes the winner. A time limit may have to be set for the course to ensure that competitors do not merely walk; or walking can be barred.

MUSICAL CHAIRS. There are two variations of this. Perhaps the most common version in this country is to form stalls out of hurdles, alternately facing different ways. When the music stops the riders find that there is one too few; the rider who has not ridden into a stall leaves the ring and one of the stalls is taken away. But a variation of this comes nearer the original children's game. Chairs are used, and the players ride round an outer circle. When the music stops they must *immediately* dismount, lead their horses to the chairs and sit down. The game proceeds in the same way.

Most commonly sacks are used and the riders must dismount and stand on a sack.

TROUSER THIEF. This is another variation on the theme of Musical Chairs. In the centre of the arena there is a pile of trousers, one less pair than there are riders. When the music stops or the ▮▮▮ blows, competitors who have been riding round an o▮▮▮ ▮▮mount, run to the centre and put on a pair of ▮▮▮uld be outsizes and have no buttons or braces, so that the▮ ▮o be held up with the hands. Once a rider has got his trousers on *and mounted his horse*, he is safe, but until he is on horseback the competitor who has no trousers can try to get them away from him. The trouserless competitor is out of the game. All the trousers but one pair are returned to the centre and the game continues.

HANDKERCHIEF STEEPLECHASE. Competitors enter this race in pairs. Each pair has to hold a handkerchief in their inside hands. If anyone lets go of the handkerchief the partner must stop and that pair are either disqualified or subjected to a penalty.

LE JEU DE ROSE

This famous game deserves a section to itself. It can be played in

This is fun as an ordinary game to teach initiative to a group of young riders as they catch their partner and remove the handkerchief or 'rose bouquet'. In formal circumstances it is performed to music by three riders who try to gather the bouquet. They are usually three gentlemen, and the bouquet is presented to a favoured lady.

a riding school, manège, at a gymkhana or in a circus ring. Those who patronized the Christmas Circus at the Crystal Palace before it was burnt down may remember the Carré Brothers performing this in the 1930s. It is advisable to ride on a snaffle only.

The game is played by three riders: (1) the wearer, who carries a bouquet on his left shoulder (or a handkerchief round his right arm); (2) the attacker, who tries to get hold of the bouquet, but who must always accomplish this *from the right* (in the case of a handkerchief, from the left); (3) the defender, whose job is to protect the wearer and keep the attacker away.

The defender, therefore, tries to place himself between the wearer and the attacker. Players should not consider this game as a kind of race, as they so often do. The wearer should taunt the attacker, challenging him to pluck the bouquet and then, instead of running away, he should turn so that the attacker is on the wrong side. The game consists of three rounds of two or three minutes each, with a rest in between.

When the attacker succeeds in capturing the bouquet or handkerchief, he, as winner of that bout, becomes the wearer in the next game; the wearer becomes the defender and the defender becomes the attacker.

Part Four

TRICK-RIDING AND VOLTIGE

INTRODUCTION
SYLVIA STANIER

Voltige, or vaulting on horseback, is fast becoming a popular sport in Great Britain. It has been a gymnastic sport in Continental Europe for a long time. It was popular with the cavalry units of both the Continental and the British armies between the wars.

Horse sports of this type have long been popular. Bareback riding was practised by the Cossacks, and they still have some of the finest vaulting and bareback riders in the world. The Mexican Indians, not long after Cortez captured Mexico for the Spaniards in the fifteenth century, found that riding horses bareback was fun, and they played games on them. Acrobatics and the sophisticated ballet on horseback (with the ballerina in full ballet costume) are spectacular versions of bareback and trick riding seen in circuses. It is believed that these acts were introduced to circus in about 1843 — at Philip Astley's famous amphitheatre; although like so many other equestrian disciplines they obviously emanated from an earlier age. Today the participants are more likely to come from the local Riding Club or Pony Club. There is now a British Vaulting Association and of course various societies abroad, particularly in Germany.

Vaulting is a healthy and courage-building sport, allowing young people to show their prowess and athleticism in what might be called an 'Olympian' way. It is used to develop balance, as well as to develop muscles. The Riding for the Disabled Group use vaulting in certain circumstances to encourage their pupils to develop their limbs, to learn balance and to enjoy sitting on a horse or pony. Team work combined with healthy exercise and athletic ability are the goals.

A word of warning here: as in everything else, proceed slowly — *festina lente*. Do not try complicated exercises before you have mastered the basics and built up your muscles systematically. In fact, it is quite a good idea to attend a local gymnastic group to learn how to become fit, and also to learn some of the exercises used, as many of these are the same as those used on

Kurtze iedoch gründliche
Beschreibung

Des Voltiger/

So wohl auf den Pferde als über
den Tisch.

Darinnen gehandelt wird von allen Sprüngen/
als in Sattel zu springen/wieder herauß/ Rever, Droicts, halben
Pomaden, halben Pomaden mit der Rever, gantzen Pomaden, Verwechseln/ anderthalb Pomaden, Beinsprin-
gen/etc. wie solches heutiges Tages in Gebrauch.

In Verlegung deß Autoris.

Mit mehren Lectionen und sehr vielen
Kupffern abgebildet.

von

Johann Georg Paschen/
F. M. Pagen Hoffmeistern.

Hall in Sachsen/
Druckts Melchior Oelschlegel.

*Title page of a seventeenth-century
German manual on vaulting.*

Theatre Royal, Covent Garden.

CHRISTMAS SEASON, 1885-6 Mr. WILLIAM HOLLAND, Manager.

GREAT
INTERNATIONAL CIRQUE.

Programme.

PRICE THREEPENCE.

horseback. It is not something you can do entirely on your own. Remember, too, that disabled vaulters should always be under the supervision of a qualified 'vaulting' or 'riding' person. For safety reasons, hard hats are required in most equestrian sports, but while in some cases — with a disabled vaulter, for example — back and chest protectors are essential, in competitive vaulting protectors and headgear may impede movement and cause injury. On a more cheerful note, vaulting is excellent for creating the feel of rhythm and keeping time when working to music.

Lijsen describes the exercises very clearly, and refers briefly to the type of horse required. He emphasizes that the animal should be obedient on the lunge and canter 'to order'. These are pre-requisites for any vaulting horse, so I refer the reader back to the chapters on Liberty work: the beginnings and how to get a horse going well on the lunge line. Lijsen also deals with trick riding — an offshoot of voltige, including such things as picking up a handkerchief off the ground while cantering past it.

(opposite) Ballet on horseback, from a Victorian circus programme. (Courtesy of Jonathan King)

An excellent type of horse to use for vaulting. Alexis Gruss and Marie Pierre Benac of Circus Gruss at the Circus World Championships in London. (David Jamieson)

Horses should be about 15 to 15.2 hands, ponies approximately 13 to 14 hands, with calm temperaments, nice comfortable canters (rather short striding) and good broad backs. In the circus world the Belgian 'rosin backs' are popular because of their conformation and temperament. Circus people often work their vaulting 'shows' as a team, showing several horses together – or several vaulters on one horse. If you are showing several horses at a time it is a good idea to have a 'lead' horse which sets the pace and the other horses follow. Nothing is worse than a horse which goes too fast or too slow. Timing when vaulting is the essence of success.

A point I have not mentioned is that a vaulting horse has to go so well on the lunge line that he can be let off it, working to command with just the bridle, roller and side-rein, usually on an enclosed circle of about 20 m. (The circus ring, remember, is 42 ft 6 in. or 13 m in diameter.) Suitable vaulting tack can be obtained via vaulting societies, or your saddler may be able to help.

TRICK-RIDING AND VOLTIGE

Voltige is simply a form of gymnastics performed either on or at the side of a trotting or preferably cantering horse. It is an excellent way of obtaining a firm seat, without relying on stirrups or reins, and of learning to keep one's balance at all times.

The first requirement is a good horse, trained for the work. Not enough attention is paid to this. Generally any horse is put on a lunge; a voltige surcingle — usually called a 'roller' in the circus — is strapped round him; and he is made to gallop in a circle. The pupil is then expected to vault on and off. This is not good enough. A voltige horse must:

(a) canter steadily with short even paces;
(b) keep a strict tempo the whole time;
(c) remain perfectly quiet whatever may happen on his back;
(d) never change foot even when the rider jumps on and off;

Change foot, i.e. change leg.

(e) gradually increase speed when the whip is moved from his tail towards his head, and slow up when the whip is held in front of him;
(f) break into a canter immediately the word 'off' is spoken, and the whip moved in a tail-to-head direction.

Before training a horse to fulfil these requirements, we must first select a quiet horse of medium height with a broad, flat back. Thin horses with narrow withers are no good for voltige work. The bearing reins should be just tight enough to keep the horse under control.

See pp. 7, 22–3 and 89–92 for discussion of bearing reins and side reins.

First he is taught to walk on the left rein. As soon as he understands that he must walk quietly round in a circle (the diameter of a classic circus ring is 42 ft) we coax him into a gentle trot. Then we teach him first to walk, then to trot, then walk again, and stop. When this is thoroughly understood he is made to canter. At this juncture it does not matter *how* he canters. His action may be too quick, too slow or too ragged: the great thing is that he should canter *to order*.

The horse with vaulting roller and side reins correctly adjusted. The rider holds the hand grips in the standard position. (Peter Hogan)

Hand grip on vaulting roller when seated normally.

The trainer stands at the centre of the ring, moving in a small circle which should not be more than a yard in diameter. He must already have learnt to use his ring-whip correctly (see *Training Horses at Liberty*). If it is necessary to touch the horse with the whip, the thong should just flick the near shoulder.

Before bringing the horse into the ring it is as well to see that the buckles on the roller are in good condition and that the holes in the straps are not torn. You must also be sure that it does not pinch.

A piece of felt or sheepskin can be used on the withers or behind the top joint of the forelegs when necessary, to prevent chafing. If the horse has a sore patch, the sheepskin should be cut away so that neither it nor the roller touches the place.

The bearing reins should be of equal length so that the horse is kept to the track. If his pace is found to be too long, or he canters too fast, the bearing reins should be shortened, but this must be done gradually.

When the horse thoroughly understands the commands — even if he does not yet canter perfectly — the trainer should mount and ride him through the exercises. If the horse canters badly, the rider pulls the off bearing rein until the horse drops back into a trot and starts again. Any improvement is rewarded, but the horse should never be allowed to drop back into a walk.

Now is the time to insist on a short even pace by gradually tightening the bearing reins and by repeatedly making him break into a canter.

As these exercises are difficult for a horse, we must see that he gets frequent spells of rest so that he can recover his breath. The first lessons should be kept short; but as the training continues they can be increased, always watching the horse's wind to see that he is not being overstrained.

Let us suppose that the horse now canters correctly. We can therefore bring in the voltige rider. He should stand behind the trainer in the middle of the ring and at first do no more than run up to the horse and take a few steps alongside and then run back. By repeating this he will teach the horse to remain unperturbed by a rider running beside him.

Except for the roller the horse is bare-backed; so carries no saddle cloth. If a felt or sheepskin is used under the roller it should not stick out either in front or behind the surcingle. Next, we must dust the horse's back with rosin and rub it in. This is the reason that horses used in voltige and jockey acts in the circus are so often light coloured; the rosin does not show. It is also the reason why ring horses are known as 'rosin-backs'.

The roller has three hand grips, one on either wither and one in between. It also has two loops of leather, one on each side at the height of the rider's foot. These are called *staffes* in the circus, and they should be large enough to allow the foot to pass right through.

A voltige horse always moves round the ring in an anticlockwise direction, that is *on the near rein*. If you have no ring, you must keep him on the lunge. The trainer remains in the middle of the

The normal rate of a horse's breathing is 8 to 16 breaths per minute. To check this watch either the nostrils or the flanks of the horse to see how quickly they are working.

Nowadays competitive vaulters often use sheepskin under the roller, and neat padded saddle cloths across the horse's back.

Rosin (resin) is a sticky white powder scattered on the horse's rump to allow the vaulter to maintain his foothold. It is derived from oil extracted from certain conifer and orange trees, and can be obtained at most good chemists.

The vaulting roller is a standard piece of equipment, as described. The person learning to vault should take expert advice on how to use the loops or 'staffes' so as not to insert the foot or leg too far in, as that would be dangerous.

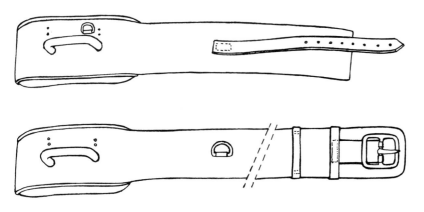

The vaulting roller from both sides, and a staffe for the foot.

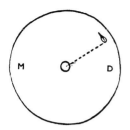

100 Points for mounting (M) and dismounting (D).

The Riding Machine is used to stop a vaulter from falling off. The horse's handler does not control the rope or pulley, which is done by an assistant. It is not always a practical piece of equipment and is difficult to acquire.

101 A safety lunge, or American Riding Machine.

The American Riding Machine in use in 1884 at Sangers in London. (Courtesy of David Jamieson)

ring to 'keep the horse up', and his pupils walk behind him. A place should be selected on the circumference of the ring for mounting and, diametrically opposite, a place fixed for dismounting. (See M and D in Fig. 100.) These positions should be *strictly* adhered to. The trainer, as he walks round in a small circle at the centre of the ring should always be on a radius which leads to the horse's tail. When several people are learning voltige at the same time, the trainer raises his whip so that each in turn can pass under it to meet the horse at the mounting point. The horse should always make a half circle without a rider, between the dismounting and mounting points.

If the ring is in an indoor riding school, or it can be otherwise contrived, it is advisable to use a safety lunge (Fig. 101). In the circus this is sometimes called a 'mechanic', or American Riding Machine, since it is said to have been invented by an American circus proprietor, Spencer Q. Stokes, about a hundred years ago. It is extremely efficient but very simple. The pupil wears a belt which has a ring at the back. One end of a rope is fastened by a swivel clip to this ring: the other leads up over a pulley and down to the trainer at the centre of the ring. The pulley must also be able to turn freely so that it always faces the moving horse. The rope should be kept just taut enough to allow the pupil the maximum freedom. When the lesson is over, before hoisting the apparatus out of the way, a small weight is fastened to the swivel clip so that it can be easily lowered when next

required. This device makes training perfectly safe and gives the pupil confidence.

All leaps and movements should first be fully explained with a standing horse, then practised at the trot and finally when cantering. But a pupil should never be forced to attempt anything of which he is the slightest bit afraid.

MOUNTING

The first thing to learn is how to mount and dismount correctly. Only too often does one see a would-be voltige rider run at his horse's side, level with the withers, body inclined towards the horse so that his left shoulder is in front of his right, and when he mounts he lands on the horse's back and pulls on the hand grips to get himself forward. This is all wrong. The rider must understand that if he makes his leap when his feet are level with the horse's withers, the horse must travel forward while he is moving vertically in the air and it is therefore impossible for him to land on the withers: he is bound to land further back on the quarters.

The correct angle of approach and the leap for mounting. Patrick Gruss. (David Jamieson)

102 Running at the horse's side before mounting.

103 Preliminary jump forward before mounting.

104 Correct position when mounted.

When running at the horse's side, as in Fig. 102, he must jump forward before leaping up (see Fig. 103). In this preliminary jump both feet should come down together, level with the horse's near leg as it touches the ground. The voltige rider then jumps off both feet and so lands astride the withers. When sitting on his horse's back his legs should hang loosely down (Fig. 104).

DISMOUNTING

In dismounting the pupil should lean slightly back, the right leg is then thrown over the neck of the horse (Fig. 105), the hands letting go and seizing the grips again in turn, in order to let the leg pass (Fig. 106). As both legs move towards the ground they should be swung forward together and land as shown in Fig. 107.

Mounting and dismounting must be practised until the movements are made perfectly. No other trick should be taught until

105 Preparation for dismounting: right leg over the horse's neck.

106 Preparation for dismounting: right leg passes under left hand.

107 Dismounting with feet together.

this has been achieved. When mounting and dismounting are performed quickly and neatly, the movements should be rehearsed to the rhythm of the horse's canter. First: 1, 2, 3, up; 1, 2, 3, down. Next this should be shortened to 1, 2, up; 1, 2, down; then 1, up; 1, down. Finally, when this can be performed with ease and grace, the feet swinging forward in dismounting to meet the ground give the necessary elevation for the leap up again, which follows immediately.

ON BOTH KNEES

For this trick the pupil, sitting astride the horse, should start by leaning forward so that his hands on the grips take the weight, then throw both legs outstretched, up backwards as *high as he can*. As the feet reach the highest point they are brought together, but the legs open again as the body falls to regain the sitting position. This should be practised on a standing horse first, then at the walk, next at the trot and finally at the canter. A safety lunge will help.

When this can be successfully accomplished the pupil keeps his knees together when his legs have reached the top of the swing and brings them forward so that he lands with his knees on the horse's quarters. The shins should follow the line of the crupper,

Kneeling on one knee. (Bob Langrish)

If the pupil kneels in the correct position the knee should lie flat on the horse's rump and should not dig in. An expert should demonstrate this.

108 Kneeling on both knees. Note the position of the feet.

109 Kneeling on one knee.

110 The scissors.

but the feet, which remain close together, should not dig into the rump (Fig. 108). Before dismounting, the legs are thrown high in the air again and open to come down astride the horse. Dismounting then proceeds in the usual way.

ON ONE KNEE

This trick is learnt in the same way as that previously described, but the right leg remains stretched out and held horizontally, so that the rider lands on his left knee (Fig. 109). His back should be horizontal and his head held well up.

THE LEG PASS

The pupil, sitting astride, throws his right leg over the horse's neck as if to dismount, but as soon as the leg reaches the near side he leans on both grips and passes the right leg under the left and back over the horse's quarters to regain the astride position. This movement should be practised until the rider can repeat it half a dozen times straight off, so that the right leg makes a non-stop series of circles.

TURNING ROUND

In this trick both legs are thrown high and outstretched in the air, as for kneeling, but the legs are crossed at the top of the swing so that the left leg falls on the off side and the right leg falls on the near side. As the legs come down the rider lets go of the grip so that his body follows its natural movement and turns to face the tail. The hands are immediately placed in front of the body on the horse's crupper. He then throws his left leg up and over the horse's neck, letting his left shoulder follow in the same direction so that he turns left about and lands in the ring on both feet, beside the horse and facing the direction in which it is moving. The best moment to dismount is when the horse raises his forehand, for the movement helps the rider.

THE SCISSORS

The rider, sitting with both legs on the near side of the horse (rather as if he were riding side-saddle), maintains his hold of the hand grips, but swings his left leg up and over the horse's crupper so that his legs are astride the horse but, as in the last trick, face the tail. Here, however, the body does not follow the legs round, since the hold on the hand grips prevents it from

Position in the air in both turning round and the scissors. (Peter Hogan)

facing more than inwards (Fig. 110). After this position has been held for a little time the hands can be moved to the crupper and the movement finished as above.

FORWARD SWING

The pupil kneels on both knees, but holds the grips so that his fingers face outwards. He then places his right shoulder in front of the roller, letting his head drop down as far as possible on the near side of the horse's neck. Next he throws his legs high up and over so that he lands in the ring on his left foot, which should be a little in front of the right. For the first lessons an assistant, leading the horse, should take the place of a lunge. If afterwards a lunge is used, great care should be taken to see that enough room is left for the swing.

This movement can also be made inwards, the rider starting with both feet on the off-side of the horse; and also backwards, in which case he lands behind the tail.

NECK AND SHOULDER STAND

The movements here are similar to the forward swing, but the rider does not hold the grips, he tucks his fingers under the rear

In other words the hands should be palm upwards when they hold the grips.

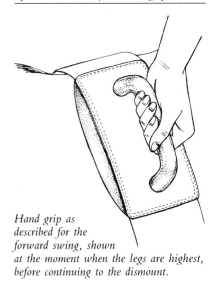

Hand grip as described for the forward swing, shown at the moment when the legs are highest, before continuing to the dismount.

A version of the neck and shoulder stand, with the hands remaining on the grips and the shoulder behind the roller. (Peter Hogan)

edge of the roller. When his right shoulder rests on the base of the horse's neck, he throws his legs up and holds them straight in a vertical position.

NEAR-SIDE MOUNT

This is made in the same way as mounting astride, but the right leg is not thrown over the horse's back, both legs remain on the near side, as if one were riding side-saddle.

OFF-SIDE MOUNT

In this movement both legs are thrown over the back of the horse and remain on the off side.

SADDLE LEAP

The rider runs alongside the horse, his right hand resting on the horse's near quarter. He then makes a high jump, taking off with his left leg; when he reaches the highest point he swings his right leg forward over the neck of the horse to land astride.

Transversal from near foot-hold. Cossack riders at Devon County Show. (Bob Langrish)

TRANSVERSAL *(from off foot-hold)*

The right foot is placed in the off *staffe*. The rider, putting his weight on the right foot, lets go of the left grip and flings his left leg over first the crupper and then over his right leg, turning his body as he goes so that he lies with his back across the bottom of the horse's neck. The top part of the body is lowered down towards the ground and the left arm stretched towards the sawdust.

PICKING UP HANDKERCHIEFS

This should first be done at a walk and then at a canter. The rider takes four handkerchiefs, with a stone knotted in one or more corners of each to prevent them from blowing away. These are carried in the left hand, while each hand holds its grip on the roller. Putting his weight on the grips the rider flings both legs up and back, bringing them down together on the off side of the horse so that he is sitting facing the outside of the ring. One foot is placed through the *staffe* and the rider leans over backwards into the ring, head downwards. He now drops the handkerchiefs at equal distances apart, seizes the near grip with his left hand and pulls himself up. He rides once round with his legs still on the off side, then lowers himself once more into the position previously described to pick the handkerchiefs up. The free leg should be held straight and high. If the rider prefers he can hold on to the near grip with his right hand, during this act.

TRICKS WITH MORE THAN ONE RIDER MOUNTING

The first rider runs up to the horse and mounts, the other waits in the centre of the ring. When his turn comes he runs to the mounting point, seizes the left grip with his left hand and with his right takes hold of the right hand of the first rider, who offers it from behind his back, and then helps him up. If there are more riders, each mounts in the same way, using the hand of the last rider. When dismounting, the last pupil to mount leans backward, raises his right leg and brings it over the other riders, who duck out of the way, and jumps off.

First rider mounting, with second rider in preparation. (Peter Hogan)

POSITIONS FOR TWO AND THREE RIDERS

Here are some positions for more than one rider:

1. The first rider lies across the neck of the horse, head downwards towards the ring, while the second rider kneels on one knee with the other leg outstretched.
2. The first rides with both legs on the near side, the second with both legs on the off side.
3. The first rides astride, facing ahead, while the second turns round so that they are riding back to back. In this the first rider dismounts before the second.
4. The first sits and the second stands.
5. The first rides astride, the second kneels on both knees while a third stands, resting his hands on the shoulders of the second. Here the third dismounts from a standing position by throwing his right leg over the kneeling rider and jumping to the ground, the second drops down to the astride position and dismounts in the ordinary way, as does the first rider.

GIVING A PERFORMANCE

When presenting a voltige act before the public, we must be sure that the horse is perfectly trained and will on no account try to

Patrick and Alexis Gruss, standing on the horse at canter with no lunge or side reins. (David Jamieson)

jump out of the ring. The various leaps and movements should be arranged so that they not only introduce maximum variety but also build up to a climax.

The instructor remains walking round the small circle at the centre of the ring, while the riders follow him round in order of their proficiency, the best last and the least proficient first.

Remember to mount and dismount at the selected points. After dismounting the rider runs immediately to the centre of the ring allowing the horse to complete half a turn without a rider. When he arrives at the centre the next rider runs to mount, passing under the instructor's whip.

ROUTINE FOR FOUR RIDERS

Single acts

1. A mounts and dismounts in quick time (1−1) once round the ring.
    B mounts and rides round the ring on both knees. Dismounts.
    C mounts and rides once round on one knee, and then once round changing knees, taking particular care to see that the other leg is outstretched. Dismounts.
    D mounts and turns, dismounts; mounts and turns again, dismounts.

2. A mounts, turns completely round, regains the astride position, rides with both legs on the off side, throws both legs over to the near side and dismounts.
    B mounts so that he lands on both knees. Dismounts.
    C mounts and lands so that both legs fall on the off side. Dismounts.
    D mounts and turns at the same time, so he lands facing the tail. Dismounts.

3. A mounts and places four handkerchiefs in the ring. Dismounts.
    B mounts and picks up the handkerchiefs and dismounts.
    C mounts and performs a forward swing.
    D mounts and performs a shoulder stand on the neck. Dismounts.

Combined acts

1. A mounts. B mounts. A rides balancing on both knees. B rides behind him balancing on one knee.

2. C mounts with both legs to the off side. D mounts with both legs to the near side. D dismounts. C dismounts.

3. *A* mounts. *B* mounts and stands behind *A*. *A* and *B* dismount together.

4. *C* mounts and lies across the horse's neck, head down in the ring. *D* mounts and rides balancing on one knee. *D* dismounts. *C* dismounts.

5. *A* mounts. *B* mounts behind him. *C* mounts behind *B*. *D* mounts behind *C*. *D* stands and then jumps off. *C* dismounts. *B* dismounts. *A* dismounts.

When dismounting the riders, all except the last, throw their right leg high in the air to the front and the remaining riders duck their heads.

OTHER ACTS

There are two further circus acts which, if they cannot be strictly classed as voltige because they contain no vaulting, cannot be included in a book on carrousels and manœuvres because they are performed standing on a horse's back. The first is the Courier of St Petersburg, sometimes billed as *Le Courrier de la Poste*, *Le Postillon de Longjumeau* or even Chico's Post. But although the Courier may denote the first stage in the link between the circus ring and the show ring, it will be dealt with last because it is more difficult to perform; for in spite of the greater control that can be gained in a 42-ft circle of sawdust, the horses can in no way be harnessed together. So first let us deal with Roman Games.

ROMAN GAMES

This is a very good act, *if it is well rehearsed*. You need two horses for each rider, evenly matched and with flat quarters. They are bridled with snaffle bits and bearing reins which, to start with, are kept two holes shorter on the near side in order to keep the horses on the circular track of the ring. When they have learnt this, the bearing reins are made equal. It is as well to couple the horses together with a short length of cord, with a swivel clip at the ends, joining the inside snaffle ring of one horse to the girth or surcingle of the other, so that the horses shall travel at the same speed. A second short strap also connects the inside snaffle rings, or the backs of the nosebands.

The rider, who should wear rubber-soled boots *without heels*, stands with one foot on the croup – not the withers – of each

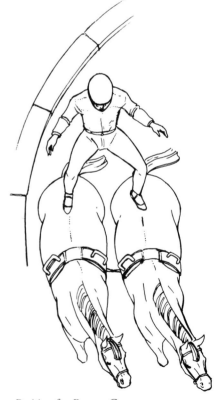

Position for Roman Games, showing coupling at the roller, as a variation from coupling between bit and roller.

Dany César, Roman riding at Austen Brothers Circus. (Bob Langrish)

horse. To help him keep his balance he can use a rein fastened to the girth of the outside horse. A safety lunge should also be used during the initial stages of training; and the croups should be well dusted with rosin.

During the first lessons an assistant can give the pupil extra confidence by walking on the near side and holding up a broom handle for the rider to grasp, if he feels himself losing his balance.

The rider enters the ring astride the inside horse and holding the bearing rein of the outside horse in his right hand. At the order 'On!' he first kneels on both knees and then quickly rises to a standing position straddling the horses. He should try to keep his balance by using his knees throughout: he should *not* move his body back and forth. Riding on the near rein, his right foot should be a little in front of his left. Such is the basis of the act known as Roman Games; the rest is formation riding.

The following routine is one which was performed in Holland by four boys, the sons of local farmers, on young horses. The descriptions are given for a rectangular arena, such as a show ring, because it is easier to follow, but it can easily be adapted for the circus ring. Further explanations of formation riding, which does not entail standing upright on a horse's back, will be found in *Carrousels and Other Equestrian Manœuvres*.

Four pairs of horses entered, one behind the other, on the right rein — that is with the near-side horse close to the fence on the long side of the arena opposite the grandstand. The riders were astride the near-side horses. At the command 'On!', they broke into a trot and, leaping up, straddled their two horses in a standing position, one foot on the crupper of each horse.

At the order 'Right — turn!' each pair of horses immediately turned right, not waiting to reach the position at which the previous horse turned, for the command then would have been 'Right — wheel!' At 'Right — turn!' therefore, the horses turned across the ring, travelling towards the grandstand *in line abreast*. A repeat of the same order brought them in line ahead, in reverse order, though still on the right rein, travelling round the arena. A repeat of this manœuvre, i.e. two right turns, brought the riders back in the correct order, still on the off rein. This was quickly followed by 'Singly — circle!' This meant that each pair of horses turned in a small circle to the right.

At the next command 'Grand figure of eight — wheel!' the riders wheeled right following the diagonal which led from the

The rider, with one foot on each horse, flexes his knees so as to absorb the movements of the horses and to keep his own balance.

An extension of Roman riding with multiple horses and riders. The Carolis go on to form a human pyramid. (David Jamieson)

entrance to the far corner of the grandstand. Here they wheeled left along the short side, left again along the other diagonal to the near corner of the grandstand. Here a right wheel brought them towards the point at which the movement had been started.

For the next movement 'Change along the diagonal!' they again wheeled diagonally across the arena towards the far corner of the grandstand and then left along the short side, but on coming to the corner, instead of moving down the other diagonal, they rode along the long side opposite the grandstand on the near rein.

A left turn took them across the arena, towards the spectators, in line abreast and another left turn at the far side brought them into line ahead in reversed order. Again a repeat of this manœuvre restored the correct order. In front of the stand the order to circle singly was given.

'Grand circle — wheel!' was the next command. In this they followed the leader in a circle as large as the arena would allow, still moving anti-clockwise.

'Pairs, at a distance', meant that the riders spaced themselves evenly round the circle. As they came on to the centre lines of the sides of the arena the order 'Odd numbers — change!' was given. Number 1 and number 3 then rode straight along the diameter of the circle to change places. The order in which they circled thus became 3, 2, 1, 4. After another circuit the order 'Even numbers — change!' made numbers 2 and 4 change places, and so the order was restored to normal.

At the command 'Four — abreast!' the first rider continued riding in a big circle, the second came up on his near side, the third on the near side of the second and the fourth on the near side of the third, turning a circle near the centre of the arena.

'Circle and change!' led to the order in line abreast being changed, as they rode round the big circle. In other words, number 1, who had been on the outside of the circle with 2, 3 and 4 on his near side, now found himself on the inside of the circle with 2, 3 and 4 on his off side. Still circling in line abreast, the command was given to 'follow the track', when they broke the circle and rode still in line abreast towards the end of the arena. A turn brought them into line ahead, following the long side opposite the grandstand. A further turn brought them all moving in line abreast towards the spectators where they halted and took their bow.

The essence of such a performance is perfect precision.

THE COURIER OF ST PETERSBURG

Here the rider makes his appearance riding two horses, straddling their cruppers, as in Roman Games; but the horses may not be

The Courier of St Petersburg. Franco Knie and Mary-José Knie of the Swiss National Circus. (David Jamieson)

Building up the number of horses in the Courier of St Petersburg. Patrick Gruss at Robert Brothers Circus. (David Jamieson)

Chico's Post. The Hungarian Herdsmen at the Horse of the Year Show. (Bob Langrish)

attached in any way, for the idea is that other horses — as many as you like — should canter into the ring singly and pass between the first two horses, under the legs of the rider, who snatches up the rein as each passes beneath him. The reins must obviously be of the right length, and the horses must come in the right order. They represent the countries over which a courier would have to travel, and in the old days bore the flags of these various nations. There are variations on this theme. In Chico's Post, for instance, three horses are driven abreast in front of the two straddled by the performer. But the basic movement, in which a horse passes between two others and beneath the rider, remains the same. In the circus ring one can sometimes see a courier driving eight horses tandem fashion, straddling three, while a twelfth pirouettes behind.

Andrew Ducrow's Courier.

It is the only one of Andrew Ducrow's acts that is still seen in the circus ring today.

The Courier of St Petersburg was invented by Andrew Ducrow, a famous English circus rider who achieved his highest success in the first half of the last century; and originated the phrase 'Cut the cackle and get to the horses'.

GLOSSARY

Aids   Help, in the form of signals to the horse by the rider or trainer, with leg or hand movements or the voice (natural aids), or such things as whips and martingales (artificial aids).

A la flèche   This is a variation on tandem riding (qv) when more than one horse is driven in front of a single ridden horse. When there are three harnessed abreast in front it is known as a troika, but with, say, four or five in front it is known as *à la flèche*.

Allez   Go (Fr.), used as a command in Liberty work to indicate that the horse should move forward.

Assistant   A helper is extremely important in teaching difficult movements and/or tricks, and should be someone who remains calm and works well with the trainer. See Part I.

Auxilliary reins   These include martingales and running reins; for the special rein designed by Lijsen see pp. 88–9.

Bearing rein   A subsidiary rein from the bit via headpiece to saddle or pad which helps to keep the horse's head at a high angle, usually used in harness horses. This term is used throughout Part I of Lijsen's work to refer to side reins (qv). But see pp. 91–2.

Carrousel   A gathering of riders showing off their horses in a formal manner, very popular in France in the eighteenth and nineteenth centuries. Now normally refers to a musical ride or quadrille.

Changez   Change direction (Fr.); used as a command in Liberty work indicating that the horse should cross the ring and continue in the opposite direction.

Collection   The gathering and containing of the horse's energy by the rider, by use of the various aids (qv).

Counter canter   The horse canters on the so-called 'wrong' (outside) leg, and is bent towards the leading leg.

Counterchange   A movement whereby the horse changes direction from side to side in a lateral position, for example in half-pass 5 m to the right of the centre line and 5 m back (see pp. 70–1).

Counterlead   At the canter, where the leading leg is the outside one rather than the inside as normal (see Counter canter).

Coupling   A strap attached at each end to the snaffle bit rings and running behind the horse's chin.

Croup   The top of the horse's quarters from loin to tail.

Crupper   A leather loop passed under the tail and attached to the saddle or roller (qv) to prevent it from slipping forward.

Cue   An aid given by the trainer, including the position of the whip and body and voice commands.

Curb chain   Chain or strap passing under the horse's chin as part of the double bridle, which consists of a bridoon (or snaffle) bit and a curb bit.

Demi-pirouette   See Pirouette.

FEI   Fédération Equestre Internationale, the international governing body of equestrian sports, based in Berne, Switzerland.

Full pass   See Pass.

Guider   A long stick (often the butt end of a lunge whip) used to instruct the horse, by signals, as to what he should do in Liberty work, i.e. turn, stop etc.

Half-pass   A collected school movement whereby the horse moves sideways, but still manages to progress forwards. See Pass, and p. 69.

Ho, Hova   A continental expression of German or Scandinavian origin for instructing the horse to stop.

Hobbles   Leather straps which surround the horse's fetlock, often used to hitch two legs together to prevent a horse from straying, but here used as a training aid.

Jambette   When the horse stands with a foreleg raised, and pivots round on the other foreleg which remains on the ground (or pedestal) with the hind quarters performing a circle. See Turn on the Forehand.

Kür   (Ger.) A free-style dressage class often performed to music.

Leg-yielding   A form of lateral work, where the horse moves forwards and sideways, looking away from the direction in which he is moving. The most basic of all lateral movements. See p. 59.

Martingale   There are two types in general use, the standing and the running, as well as many variations. They are used to control the horse's head carriage. When Lijsen refers just to a 'martingale', he means a running martingale. See p. 87.

Movement   Word used to describe a specific action such as a circle; not in this case movement of direction or locomotion.

Pas de deux   When two riders perform an integrated programme.

Pass   These are the half-pass and the full pass. In the former the horse progresses forwards and to the side at the same time and in the latter he progresses sideways only. (See p. 58)

Passage   A highly elevated slow trot with a period of

163

suspension between diagonals.

Pedestal   A low strong wooden box or tub, 12–15 in. high, on which the horse places its front feet. Ponies may sometimes stand on it with all four feet.

Piaffe, Piaffer   A highly elevated trot with no forward movement.

Pirouette   There are two kinds. The one done at liberty is when the horse makes a small complete circle and then proceeds on his way. In ridden work a pirouette is made in walk or canter. If in canter, it is important that the horse takes his weight well on to his hind legs and keeps the canter rhythm. A demi-pirouette is a 180° turn.

Platoon   A large musical ride may divide into sections, e.g. six riders, known as platoons.

Polka   The Spanish Walk or Trot with a three-time beat.

Race horse   A horse bred for and usually used solely for horse racing. The term usually refers to the Thorough-bred, although Arabians and Quarter Horses are also bred specifically to race.

Rein back   When a horse is asked to proceed backwards instead of forwards.

Renvers   One of the lateral movements, the inverse movement to *travers* (qv). See pp. 58, 68.

Ring-whip   A long whip used by the handler of a group of liberty horses. It has a thick, fairly long and flexible handle and a long thin leather lash (see pp. 22–3).

Roller   A piece of leather or jute approximately 4 in. wide with a buckle and straps, fastened around the body of the horse in about the same place as the saddle would sit. For voltige work a roller should have three hand grips, one on top and one on each side.

Rosin back   Horse used for bareback riding in the circus, so-called because the back of the horse is sprinkled with rosin (resin) for grip. The horses used are often Belgian Draught horses because they are sturdy and have broad backs.

Running reins   Reins which go from the rider's hands through the rings of the bit and back to the saddle. They are usually used to help lower the horse's head, and are similar to draw reins.

Serpentine   A series of half circles with a change of direction between each one. It can also refer to lateral movements of a few paces in each direction.

Shoulder-in   One of the best-known basic lateral movements, together with shoulder-out (see p. 58).

Side reins   Reins which are fixed on either side of the horse, usually from the girth straps (at mid-shoulder level) to the snaffle ring of the bit. Sometimes the reins contain a rubber inset half way along, or they may be solid leather. In either case they should be adjustable. They are used to control the position of the horse's head.

Spanish Trot   See Spanish Walk.

Spanish Walk   The horse raises and stretches each foreleg high in walk. A similar movement can also be performed at the trot, but this is more difficult. See pp. 39–41, 82–6.

Stock   The handle of a ring-whip (qv).

Tandem   Normally a driving term, here it refers to a ridden horse off which the rider drives another in front, so the horses follow one another.

Temperament   The individual character of the horse, e.g. quiet, excitable, nervous. Lijsen uses the term to mean spirit and courage.

Travers   One of the more advanced lateral movements (see pp. 58, 68).

Track-up   A term used to denote whether the hind feet of the horse when moving forwards come up to the hoof-prints left by the fore feet.

Trick   Different to movement (qv), this word denotes a specific thing such as teaching the horse to bow, to lie down or kneel. Tricks are not allowed in dressage competitions, but are usually included in circus as part of the entertainment. Lijsen sometimes uses the terms trick and movement interchangeably.

Trick rider   A person who performs tricks while riding or vaulting.

Troika   A team of three horses driven abreast. (See Tandem and *A la flèche*.)

Trotter   A breed of horse on the continent (especially France and Scandinavia) and in the USA (where it is known as a Standardbred), specifically bred for trotting races.

Turn on the forehand   A movement in which the horse's front feet stay relatively in the same place and the hind feet rotate around them (see p. 59).

Turn on the hind quarters   The exact opposite to the turn on the forehand (see p. 68), and the basis for a pirouette.

Two deep   Term to denote Liberty horses working in pairs, that is side by side.

Two tracks   Term used to denote that the horse is moving laterally.

Valsez   Waltz (Fr.); the command used to make a group of Liberty horses pair up head to tail and, by circling round together in pirouette, appear to be waltzing.

Volt, volte   A small circle, usually of 6 m in diameter.

Voltige   The exercise of vaulting on and off the horse, or gymnastics on horseback.